Readers' Responses to Kay M. Bowman's Inspirational Writings:

Kay, your words of faith and strength in the midst of your own trials are truly an inspiration to me.
—Les and Joanne Solomon, Perry, GA

Your poetry is a real gift.
—Gale and Malcolm Harlow, Berryville, VA

What a beautiful witness you are as you express so beautifully your love and appreciation of our Lord! You are gifted in expressing your innermost feelings. Your words feed my soul.
—Beth Spitler, Swoope, VA

We are utterly amazed that you write in such a poetic style! You always have just the right and colored words to give a beautiful picture in words!
—George and Nelle Fields, Decatur, GA

You need to know how very much your poetry touches my heart!
—Ann DeVeny, Hampstead, NC

You are so creative in your writing!
—Margaret Rainbolt, Bridgewater, VA

Kay, we enjoyed your poems so much!
—Richard and Carol Brock, Canadian, TX

Your poetry is wonderful! What a gift you have!
—Carol Grant, Orem, UT

Kay, I just love all your poems and am just amazed at how you put them all together in such an inspiring way!
—Gary and Dee Shuck, Moreno Valley, CA

Kay, You are such a terrific writer and inspirational poet. Thank you and may God continue to bless you and yours!
—Laura Foster, Clinton, TN

Your poetry is amazing!
—Glen and Malinda Stoltzfus, Harrisonburg, VA

Your God-given talent of such inspiring poetry is truly amazing!
—Bob Pfeil, South Park, PA

Your poetry is so beautiful and so inspiring!
—Larry and Pat Fikstad, Layton, UT

Kay, your poetry is so inspiring!
—Sue and Eric Wible, Etters, PA

Kay, your poems are so informative and original and you make me see and feel the words in your poems.
—Peggy Hammer, Bridgewater, VA

Tears Within My Heart:

by Kay M. Bowman

Copyright 2012 by Prince of Peace Press

Published by CreateSpace
Imprint Prince of Peace Press
Harrisonburg, Virginia

All rights reserved. No part of this book may be reprinted or reproduced in any form or by any electronic, mechanical or other means, now known or hereafter invented, including photocopying, recording, and information storage and retrieval, without permission in writing from the author.

Library of Congress Cataloging-in-Publication Data

Tears within my heart: A modern-day psalms collection/by Kay M. Bowman.

ISBN: 0615723144.
Printed in the United States of America.

First edition, 2013

Credits
Cover design: Darin Keith Bowman
Photo credits: Melissa Lipton
                     Ron Rammelkamp
                     Darla Kay Deardorff
                     Darin Keith Bowman
                     (Note: Prayer Shawl in front cover photo was made by women of the Bridgewater Church of the Brethren Prayer Shawl Ministry)
Production assistant: Kaylee Deardorff
Editor: Darla K. Deardorff
To contact the author, email at dkdeardorff@gmail.com

Dedication

I dedicate this book, first of all, to God, without whom the book would have been impossible. My constant prayer to God was that He must be the writer, editor, publisher, and marketer–that I am "His servant in writing" and that the publishing must be according to His will. I thank God for His enduring love, mercy, and grace when many things hindered my writing.

To my late husband, Reverend Harold I. Bowman, who supported and encouraged me each day with his love, strength, and deep faith through our forty five years of happy marriage.

To our beloved children: daughter, Darla Kay and husband Duane; son, Darin Keith and wife Karen; and son, Devin Kent, who believed in me, encouraged me, and prayed consistently for this project.

To our grandchildren: Kaylee and Shaun Deardorff and Peyton and Carter Bowman, whose child-like wonder and never-ending interest brought comfort and happiness to me throughout this writing.

Acknowledgement

I thank God for giving me perseverance and endurance when the job seemed overwhelming, for sending me just the right word of encouragement, just the right sign of His presence when I needed it to carry on.

I acknowledge with deep gratitude all those family members, friends, and others who have encouraged me through the years to put the writings God has given to me into a book.

May God bless each of you.

—Kay M. Bowman

Table of Contents

Introduction

Chapter 1 - Prayers When I Face Trials 23

Chapter 2 - Prayers When I Am Struggling 45

Chapter 3 - Prayers in the Loss of a Loved One 65

Chapter 4 - Prayers for Deliverance 101

Chapter 5 - Prayers for Restoration 123

Chapter 6 - Prayers When I Need God's Guidance 145

Chapter 7 - Prayers When I Seek God's Leading 175

Chapter 8 - Prayers for Peace and Contentment 203

Table of Contents

INTRODUCTION	19
CHAPTER 1 - PRAYERS WHEN I FACE TRIALS	23
Affliction	24
All I Can Do Is Pray	26
Anchored to Stay	28
Blessed by Burdens	30
God's Masterpiece	32
How Many Times?	34
My Cross	36
My Hiding Place	38
Out of My Weakness	40
This Path for Me	42
CHAPTER 2 - PRAYERS FOR WHEN I AM STRUGGLING	45
Carry Life Lightly	46
Come to Him	48
Courage	50
Endurance	52
Faith	54
Faith Grows During Storms	56
Faith or Despair?	58
How Many Times?	60
Finding Jesus	62

Chapter 3 - Prayers in the Loss of A Loved One — 65
And the Robins Were There — 66
Changes — 68
Change — 70
Comforted by God — 72
Divine Appointment — 74
Going Home — 76
Going Home — 78
Is It Well? — 80
It's Raining in My Heart — 82
Let Me Run with Patience — 84
Life and Immortality — 86
Lord, Here I Am Again — 88
My Sister's Time to Die — 90
My Sister's Gone — 92
Once Again It's Spring — 94
The Rainbow — 96
The Time Has Finally Come — 98

Chapter 4 - Prayers for Deliverance — 101
A Touch of Sadness and A Promise — 102
Adversities or Opportunities? — 104
Finishers — 106
God's Discipline — 108
God's Love — 110
God's Love Endless as the Ocean — 112
Grace — 114
Immeasurable Is God's Love — 116
In Your Hands Are Strength and Power — 118
Left Alone! — 120

Chapter 5 - Prayers for Restoration — 123
My Life Is Now in Ruin, Lord — 124
It Was Love — 126
Life Is Like a Shadow — 128

Limitless Is Your Love, O Lord	*130*
New Beginnings	*132*
Only God Fills the Empty Place	*134*
My Sacred Place	*136*
Our Sufficiency Is from God	*138*
Swifter Than A Weaver's Shuttle	*140*
The Trials You Give, Lord	*142*

CHAPTER 6 - PRAYERS WHEN I NEED GOD'S GUIDANCE — 145

"But God" Moments	*146*
Called to Be Still	*148*
Being Still	*150*
Dream Your Dream	*152*
God Knows Best	*154*
God Knows Best	*156*
God's Work for Me	*158*
How Am I Answering God's Call?	*160*
How Many Times Have I Prayed Today?	*162*
If God Has Called You, "Go!"	*164*
Keep Me Humble, Lord	*166*
Keep Me, Lord	*168*
Lord, Teach Me to Be Humble	*170*
Lord, What Will You Have Me to Do?	*172*

CHAPTER 7 - PRAYERS WHEN I SEEK GOD'S LEADING — 175

My Mission	*176*
My Ways or God's?	*180*
No Deed Is Too Small	*182*
O Restless Heart	*184*
Obedience	*186*
Only My Daily Bread	*188*
Only One Moment	*190*
Only Wait	*192*
Our Lord Is in Control	*194*
People Are Watching Me	*196*

The Leaf	*198*
The Storm	*200*

CHAPTER 8 - PRAYERS FOR PEACE AND COMFORT — 203

All That I Have	*204*
All That I Need	*206*
Do I Have Peace About It?	*208*
God's Perfect Peace	*210*
Guideposts to Peace	*212*
I Shall Not Want	*214*
Living in Your Will, O Lord	*216*
Longing for You, Lord	*218*
More Than Enough	*220*
Peace	*222*
Perfect Peace	*224*
Take What Each Day Brings	*226*
The Breaking Process	*228*
The Dying Embers of the Setting Sun	*230*
You Giveth Quietness	*232*
Your Peace Is Certain, Lord	*234*

Introduction

How many times have tears filled our eyes and hearts with grief, sadness, and sorrow? How many times have we reached out for strength and comfort during our trials and suffering? Not one of us escapes suffering of some kind during our journey on earth. And God is there for us – to dry our tears, to give us encouragement to move forward, to comfort us that we might give comfort to others.

Born out of intense grief and deep pain in my own life experiences, *Tears Within My Heart* will bring comfort to your suffering spirit as you read prayers from the heart of God Himself in times of loss and struggle. Just as the Psalmist David communed with God from the deep needs of his heart on the hillsides of Judae tending sheep, so you, too, will be able to identify with the same feelings, emotions, and questions that arise within your own heart as you read these modern day Psalm prayers.

Grounded in scripture and accompanied by faith-building quotations, these prayers written in simple, easy-to-understand Psalm-like words will give you faith, hope, and encouragement as you face trials in your own journey of life. They will bring comfort, insight and inspiration during the difficult times. You will be drawn into a deeper, closer relationship with God as you receive fresh insight to scripture, food for your soul, and unmatched peace through this handbook of strength and comfort. As you are drawn into a closer relationship with God, you will find it to be a relationship that will sustain you during the hard times of life's struggles.

These modern day Psalm prayers cover all aspects of our daily living from trials and struggles, loss of loved ones, deliverance and restoration, and God's guidance to peace and contentment knowing that God's ever present spirit is always with us.

Tears Within My Heart will touch each human soul of suffering with poignancy, purpose, and power to feel God speaking comfort, courage, and compassion to their hurting heart.

Forever in His service,
Kay M. Bowman

> "Consider it pure joy whenever you face trials of many kinds because you know that the testing of your faith develops perseverance."
> – James 1:2

"To learn strong faith is to endure great trials."
– George Muller

Prayers When I Face Trials

Chapter 1

Revelations 3: 19, "Those whom I love I rebuke and discipline."

I Peter 4: 12, "Beloved, do not think it strange concerning the firey trial which is to try you, as though some strange thing happened to you."

Affliction

Help me, O Lord, to stand quietly
And endure my affliction today,
So that not only in me Your grace is revealed,
But your glory will light someone's way...

Help me to now understand and to know
That my affliction is from You alone,
That under Your direction and guidance divine,
Your grace and glory will be known...

Your trials are never by chance, O Lord,
Each one on a special mission,
Touching only the heart that it's intended for,
Bringing dependence and total submission...

So may I welcome the arrow you send
Of the trial that I am to bear,
May it be used, Lord, for Your honor and glory
As a witness with others to share.

Chapter 1 | Prayers When I Face Trials

The word "trial" is defined as a test or examination of our character. When trials come, we are to receive them with joy, recognizing a God-given opportunity to identify those specific character flaws we need to change so that we can love more purely.
—Ray and Nancy Kane, from Fear to Love (2002)

Like a rose whose fragrance is sweetest when its petals are crushed, the fragrance of Christ is made sweeter in our lives by affliction.
—Anne Graham Lotz, The Daily Light Journal (2004)

We can face any affliction when we know the Lord is with us.
—Anonymous

Tears Within My Heart | K.M. Bowman

I Thessalonians 5: 17-18, "Pray without ceasing. In everything give thanks for this is the will of God in Christ Jesus concerning you."

All I Can Do Is Pray

"All I can do, Lord, is pray!"
What a privilege from You alone
To lift my voice in prayer
And feel Your power made known...

Praying unlocks the doors of heaven
And releases Your mighty power,
You always answer my prayer,
Whether it is later or within the hour...

Whether "yes" or "no" or "wait,"
Your answer is always right,
"All I can do is pray,"
And know You will answer my plight.

Chapter 1 | Prayers When I Face Trials

God does nothing but in answer to prayer.
– John Wesley

God answers prayer with certainty. Wish fulfillment is something else.
– Anonymous

The only way to pray is to pray, and the way to pray is to pray much.
– Anonymous

The purpose of prayer is not to inform God of our needs, but to invite Him to rule our lives.
– Clarence Bauman

Keep praying, but be thankful that God's answers are wiser than your prayers.
– William Culbertson

Tears Within My Heart | *K.M. Bowman*

Job 13: 15, "Though He slay me, yet will I hope in Him."

Anchored to Stay

An old seaman once said
As he looked over the sea,
"In fierce storms that come,
There's one thing that must be...

"For there's only one way to survive
Fierce storms of the sea,
Put the ship in position
And not let it go free..."

So it is, Lord, with my spirit
When rough seas assail,
I must stand firm in You
And trust You without fail...

I must anchor myself
Steadfastly to You
When no sun lights the way,
When shadows blind my view...

Reason cannot help me,
Past experiences shed no light,
When the storm is bearing down,
To You, I hold tight...

Chapter 1 | Prayers When I Face Trials

With my soul in Your position
Then come what may–
Wind, waves or rough seas,
I am anchored to stay.

When you have no helpers, see all your helpers in God. When you have many helpers, see God in all your helpers. When you have nothing but God, see all in God; when you have everything, see God in everything. Under all conditions, stay thy heart only on the Lord.
– Charles H. Spurgeon

Job 5: 17-18 NIV, "*Blessed is the man whom God corrects; so do not despise the discipline of the Almighty. For He wounds, but He also binds up; He injures, but His hands also heal.*"

Blessed by Burdens

Out of pain have come poignant poems;
Out of problems, the sweetest songs;
Out of suffering, the greatest spirits;
Out of tears, the rights from wrongs...

From adversity have come the most blessed lives;
From harsh conditions, the most compassionate souls;
From trouble, those filled with the greatest peace;
From sorrow, those who console...

Therefore, may I find comfort in my suffering, Lord,
Find peace in my pain;
For from my trials of deepest testing
Will come rich blessings of greatest gain.

Chapter 1 | Prayers When I Face Trials

We are not here to play, to dream, to drift,
We have hard work to do and loads to lift,
Shun not the battle; face it. 'Tis God's gift.
-Maltbie D. Babcock

Tears Within My Heart | K.M. Bowman

Nahum 1: 12, "Although I have afflicted you, I will afflict you no more."

God's Masterpiece

Born in the sculptor's hand,
The masterpiece stood alone,
Enduring a thousand blows
As its shape took form in stone...

Each blow made it sharper,
Clearer, if you will,
Till the image became distinct,
And none its place could fill...

And aren't I like that, too, Lord,
In Your Master Sculptor's hand?
Enduring blows one by one
In the image You have planned?...

That I be glorified in Christ
And reflect His glory back
That others may see His likeness
And help them stay on track...

The trials will serve their purpose, Lord,
In who You want me to be,
A person of worth and beauty
In the things I cannot see...

Chapter 1 | Prayers When I Face Trials

As the next blow is received
By Your Master Sculptor's hand,
May I remember I am Your masterpiece
In the image You have planned.

When through fiery trials thy pathway shall lie,
My grace, all sufficient, shall be thy supply;
The flame shall not hurt thee; I only design
Thy dross to consume and thy gold to refine.
– George Keith

God prepares great men for great tasks by great trials.
– J. K. Gressett

Note: God's Masterpiece originally published in Messenger, 2012

Mark 6:46, "And when He had sent them away, He departed into a mountain to pray."

How Many Times Have I Prayed Today?

How many times have I prayed today, Lord?
A short little minute span?
Or is my life one continuous prayer
Around which my life is planned?

You spent much time in daily prayer,
You were never too hurried to pray,
Your example's for me to spend much time in prayer
As I go about my day...

How important it is to meet You, Lord,
With perseverance and persistence and pleading,
Knowing that You hold the only key
To what my life is needing.

Chapter 1 | Prayers When I Face Trials

Prayer is for every moment of our lives, not just for times of suffering or joy.
– Billy Graham

There is no part of religion so neglected as private prayer.
– J. C. Ryle

Mark 8:34, "If anyone would come after me, he must deny himself and take up his cross and follow me."

My Cross

My cross is the one You give me, O Lord,
May I submissive be,
May I welcome it with patience, an uncomplaining spirit,
And bear it gladly for Thee...

For through my cross, You mature my wisdom,
You deepen my inner peace,
You increase my courage, supplement my power,
Give me blessings that never cease...

Through the cross You give, though painful and distressing,
Greater use I will be to You,
For I can comfort others as You comfort me
With understanding from their point of view...

My cross is the one You give me, O Lord,
May I submissive be,
May I welcome it with patience, an uncomplaining spirit,
And bear it gladly for Thee...

Chapter 1 | Prayers When I Face Trials

Blessed is any weight, however overwhelming, which God has been so good as to fasten with His own hands upon our shoulders.
– Frederick W. Faber

God giveth the shoulder according to the burden.
– Anonymous

Tears Within My Heart | K.M. Bowman

Psalm 32: 7, "Thou art my hiding place; Thou dost preserve me from trouble; Thou dost surround me with songs of deliverance."

My Hiding Place

You are my hiding place, Lord,
With songs of deliverance, you surround me,
You are my place of refuge,
My comfort, my security...

You are my preserve from trouble,
My high mountain and my rock,
You take away my struggle, Lord,
You give me the key of peace to unlock...

You preserve me in the pressures of life,
You sustain me in the stress,
When I feel overwhelmed,
I praise You and am blessed...

For You are my hiding place, Lord,
No other can take Your place,
You are my shelter in the storm,
I will praise You all of my days.

Chapter 1 | Prayers When I Face Trials

If God is in charge and loves us, then whatever is given is subject to His control and is meant ultimately for our joy.
— Elisabeth Elliott

Hebrews 14: 34 NKJV, "Out of weakness... were made strong."

Out of My Weakness

Lord, out of my weakness,
You made me strong,
You took my waywardness
And made me belong...

You took my faults
And cleansed from within,
Out of my weakness,
You forgave me from sin...

You gave me a trial
Which was difficult to face,
But out of my weakness,
You gave me Your grace...

You closed the door
With my journey an end,
But out of my weakness,
You showed me a bend...

For Your plan was greater
Than my weakness could see,
And You led me to share
In Your ways meant to be...

Chapter 1 | Prayers When I Face Trials

No more will I say
Out of my weakness, I'm weak,
For I become strong, indeed, Lord,
When it's Your strength I seek.

Many Christians estimate difficulties in the light of their own resources, and thus attempt little and often fail in the little they attempt. All God's giants have been weak men who did great things for God because they reckoned on His power and presence being with them.
– James Hudson Taylor

Tears Within My Heart | K.M. Bowman

Hebrews 4: 16 NRSV, "Let us…approach the throne of grace with boldness, so that we may receive mercy and find grace to help in time of need."

This Path for Me

Chance has not brought
This path for me,
It is Your own hand, Lord,
In ways I can't see…

The obstacles are there,
I feel the pain,
But You have a purpose,
It is not in vain…

With each pain I feel, Lord,
You dry my tear,
And with each trial I face,
You draw me near…

I see in part;
You see in whole;
The trials I face
Are to perfect my soul..

To make me more like You
In my life each day,
To reflect Your goodness
In what I do and say…

You know the pattern
And You have the thread
To weave the light and dark
In the overall spread…

When I face the dark, Lord,
And think it cannot be,
This path that You planned
And meant for me…

I am drawn closer to You,
And hear you say,
"I will use these trials
For my glory today…

They are part of my plan
I will use them for good
To share of My love
With the whole brotherhood."

Chapter 1 | Prayers When I Face Trials

The joy and the sorrow,
The triumph and defeat
Are all woven together
To make life complete…

Pain is pain and sorrow is sorrow. It hurts. It limits. It impoverishes. It isolates. It restrains. It works devastation deep within the personality. It circumscribes in a thousand different ways. There is nothing good about it. But the gifts God can give with it are the richest the human spirit can know.
—Margaret Clarkson

> *"How long, O Lord? Will you forget me forever? How long will you hide your face from me? How long must I wrestle with my thoughts and every day have sorrow in my heart?" How long will my enemy triumph over me? But I trust in your unfailing love; my heart rejoices in your salvation. I will sing to the Lord, for he has been good to me."*
> *– Psalm 13*

"The greatest battles of life are fought out daily in the silent chambers of the soul."
– David O. McKay

Prayers When I am Struggling

Chapter 2

Tears Within My Heart | *K.M. Bowman*

Matthew 11:28 "Come unto me, all ye that labor and are heavy laden, and I will give you rest."

Carry Life Lightly

Have the strains of life made you weary and tired?
Have the burdens of life slowed you down?
Maybe you are carrying life too heavily
In the Lord peaceful rest can be found…

As my thoughts turn to You, Lord, I find You give rest
Midst the work You give me to do,
If I don't strain, don't tug, don't worry, just relax,
One job at a time gets me through…

While doing that job, I think only of it
And the fulfillment it gives serving You,
At the end of the day I feel peace in my heart,
Doing my best helps me feel renewed…

"Come unto me," You said to us all
"And I will give you much needed rest,"
"All you who labor and with care heavy laden,
I want to give you life's best…."

So may I carry life lightly from day to day, Lord,
Enjoy it, be cheerful and share
The gifts that I give along life's way
Will help others their burdens to bear.

Chapter 2 | Prayers When I am Struggling

God will never adjust His agenda to fit ours. He will not speed up His pace to catch up with ours; we need to slow our pace in order to recover our walk with Him. God will not scream and shout over the noisy clamor; He expects us to seek quietness, where His still small voice can be heard again.
– Charles Swindoll

When we live life in a hurry, we end up weary...in a hurry.
– Keri Wyatt Kent

Don't let the cares of the day, the stresses of the moment, and the worries of tomorrow interfere with your communing with and partaking of the love affair that Jesus longs for you to have with Him.
– Dee Brestin and Kathy Troccoli

Tears Within My Heart | *K.M. Bowman*

Matthew 11: 28, "Come to Me, all who are weary and heavy laden, and I will give you rest."

Come to Him

I am worn out, weary, worried,
Faced with many a trial and test,
I come to You, Lord, as I am,
For I know You will give me rest...

I am heart broken, harassed, heavy laden,
Disappointed, disillusioned, drained,
I come to You, Lord, as I am,
In You my wholeness is maintained...

I come to You with my weariness,
I come to You with my stress,
You will give me comfort and peace
And my desperately longed for rest...

This is the moment now,
The moment I will find that rest,
For You will fulfill Your promise
And in You my life will be blessed.

Chapter 2 | Prayers When I am Struggling

God never does anything to us that isn't for us.
– Elisabeth Elliot

Sometimes God gives us a gentle push of courage, sometimes He mercifully numbs us so we don't experience the full intensity of our pain, at other times He carries us when we cannot take another step on our own.
 – Bruce Carroll

Tears Within My Heart | K.M. Bowman

John 16: 33 NLT, "Here on earth you will have many trials and sorrows. But take heart, because I have overcome the world."

Joshua 1: 9, "Be strong and of a good courage; be not afraid, neither be thou dismayed; for the Lord thy God is with thee whithersoever thou goest."

Courage

Joys and sorrows, difficulties and griefs,
Come into my life each day,
Tests and trials, trauma and tragedy
Meet me each bend of the way...

But whatever happens, Lord, whatever I face,
I can hold my own soul free,
Refusing to give in or let faith be bound
By life's myriad tragedy...

By placing unshakable trust and unwavering faith
In Your goodness, Lord, that will never cease,
I am encircled with grace and Your endless love
And an aura of lasting peace.

Chapter 2 | Prayers When I am Struggling

When people see how courageous and optimistic you are during your troubled times, they will be drawn to Christ.
– Josh McDowell and Bob Hostetler

Life is essentially a series of events to be lived through rather than intellectual riddles to be played with and solved. Courage is worth ten times more than any answers that claim to be total.
– George A. Buttrick

Without courage, all other virtues lose their meaning.
– Winston Churchill

Jeremiah 45: 5, "Should you then seek great things for yourself? Seek them not. 'For I will bring disaster on all people,' declares the Lord, 'but wherever you go, I will let you escape with your life.'"

Psalm 23: 5, "...a table before You in the presence of your enemies...a shelter from the storm."

Ephesians 6: 18, "Praying always with all prayer and supplication in the spirit, and watching thereunto with all perseverance..."

Endurance

You give me endurance, O Lord,
In the presence of enemies great
Because I dwell in Your holy presence,
Within me endurance You create...

I pray for deliverance from trials
And trust You that deliverance will be,
I must also pray that You make me
What I should be in the trials that I see...

I must also pray that I'm able
To live within trials present and past,
Aware I am held by You, Lord,
No matter how long the trials may last...

You are a shelter from the storm, O Lord,

Chapter 2 | Prayers When I am Struggling

A fortress amid the foe,
A life preserved in continual pressure,
In difficulties You help me grow...

I will always be able to endure
In the presence of enemies in this land,
Because I dwell in Your holy presence
And You're with me wherever I am.

The secret of endurance is to remember that your pain is temporary, but your reward will be eternal.
– Rick Warren

Determination fades quickly without endurance.
– Steve Campbell

Romans 4: 18, "Against all hope, Abraham in hope believed."

Faith

You send Your help, Lord,
In my greatest need
That Your hand may be seen
As You intercede…

You choose this method
That I may clearly see
My trust only in You
Whatever circumstances be…

So that I depend on You
And trust only in You
For faith only works
When sight fades from view…

Faith only works
When my own prospects fail,
Then You meet my need
With Your power to prevail…

May I remember my sight
Must disappear from view
For my faith to work
As I trust in You.

Chapter 2 | Prayers When I am Struggling

Biblical faith is trusting in God, and the power of faith is putting the matter in God's hands so that He is able to do what He wants to do in that situation.
– Maurice R. Irvin

True faith drops its letter in the post office box and lets it go. Distrust holds on to a corner of it and wonders that the answer never comes.
 – A. B. Simpson

Job 23: 10, "He knows the way that I take; when He has tested me, I will come forth as gold."

Romans 8: 37, "Yet in all these things, we are more than conquerors through Him who loved us."

Faith Grows During Storms

Faith grows during storms,
Storms, too, will pass,
Faith grows during storms,
It is faith that will last…

When I meet someone, Lord,
Of great spiritual strength,
He has traveled a steep, rocky path,
A path of great length…
.
His faith grew during storms
To a victorious height,
And for my faith to grow, too,
I must walk through storms in the night…

The path of faith
Is one of victories and trials,
Of suffering and healing,
Of tears and smiles…

Chapter 2 | Prayers When I am Struggling

Of conflicts and triumphs,
Of trouble and distress,
Of hardships and dangers,
Of misunderstandings and stress...

When a storm comes my way, Lord,
I will meet you there
To give me invincible faith
That with others I might share...

So let me head straight for the center
Of the trials that I meet,
Faith grows in storms,
Proclaiming victory over defeat.

Faith never knows where it is being led, but it loves and knows the One who is leading.
– Oswald Chambers

Faith sees the invisible, believes the incredible, and receives the impossible.
 – Anonymous

Hebrews 11: 6,"Without faith, it is impossible to please God, because anyone who comes to Him must believe He exists and that He rewards those who earnestly seek Him."

Faith or Despair?

Faith holds on and prevails;
Despair gives in and fails;
Faith proclaims a victory shout;
Despair surrenders to a defeatist's doubt...

Faith triumphs in the greatest test;
Despair retreats with the smallest quest;
Faith and despair–the two shall meet–
One a winner, the other defeat.

Chapter 2 | Prayers When I am Struggling

For the believer, there is no question, for the non-believer, there is no answer.
– Anonymous

If we cannot believe God when circumstances seem to be against us, we do not believe Him at all.
– Charles H. Spurgeon

Tears Within My Heart | K.M. Bowman

Psalm 120: 1, "When I was in trouble, I called to the Lord and He answered me."

Psalm 13: "How long, O Lord? Will you forget me forever? How long will you hide your face from me? How long must I wrestle with my thoughts and every day have sorrow in my heart? How long will my enemy triumph over me? Give light to my eyes, or I will sleep in death; my enemy will say, 'I have overcome him,' and my foes will rejoice when I fall. But I trust in your unfailing love; my heart rejoices in your salvation. I will sing to the Lord, for he has been good to me."

How Many Times?

How many times did You comfort me, Lord,
In my days of sadness and sorrow?
How many hours did You bring me peace
And give me hope for tomorrow?

How often did You surround and embrace me
With Your loving arms of care?
How much did You reach out to me
In love and concern and prayer?

How many times have You guided me
Through periods of tears and despair?
How many times have You shown me "signs"
To let me know You are there?

Chapter 2 | Prayers When I am Struggling

How many times have You encouraged me
To go when the going's rough?
How many times have You picked me up
When the going was just too tough?

How often is it You give me a nudge
To try and try again?
How often do You give me the strength
To finish the work I began?

Many are the times I depend on You, Lord,
Moment by moment each day,
How many times would I fail in life
Without You to whom I could pray?

If God is the captain of our fate, our boat may rock, but it will never sink.
– Jessie Brown

The presence of Christ puts pain in perspective.
– David L. Thompson

Tears Within My Heart | *K.M. Bowman*

Romans 8: 32, "He who did not spare His own Son, but delivered Him up for us all, how shall He not with Him also freely give up all things?"

Romans 8: 31, "God is for us—you and me."

Romans 8: 38-39, "Nothing can ever separate us from the love that God imparts."

Finding Jesus

It was the year that He was missing
From the manger in the stall,
The tiny Baby Jesus,
Most important of them all...

I came home that wintry evening,
And the manger I found bare,
Someone took my Jesus
And only straw was there...

Are there times in your life, too,
When you feel that someone stole
The Christ child from your life
And the trials now take their toll?...

That circumstances difficult
Surround your life each day,
That you cannot find our Lord
Amid the trials along the way...

Chapter 2 | Prayers When I am Struggling

How can I find Jesus
When life against me seems to be?
The answer is Romans 8–
"God is for us–you and me." (Vs. 31)

"Nothing can ever separate us
From the love that God imparts," (vs. 38-39)
And I have found the Christ child
When I have Christmas in my heart.

You need to make room for God in your lives. When you do, you'll be amazed at the difference. You'll see God's hand directing you, you'll hear His voice comforting you, and you'll sense His spirit embracing you. He will be real to you.
– Bruce Bickel and Stan Jantz

> *"You will grieve, but your grief will turn to joy."*
> *– John 16:20*

"Sorrow is a fruit, God does not make it grow on limbs too weak to bear it."
– Victor Hugo

Prayers in the Loss of a Loved One

Chapter 3

Romans 15: 13 NCV, "I pray that the God who gives hope will fill you with much joy and peace while you trust in him. Then your hope will overflow by the power of the Holy Spirit."

Philippians 4: 19-20 NKJV, "And my God shall supply all your need according to His riches in glory by Christ Jesus. Now to our God and Father be glory forever. Amen."

And the Robins Were There

I was at the cemetery today
And the robins were there!
Snow on the ground!
Snow everywhere!...

Wind blowing hard!
Cold was the air!
But hope filled my heart
Because the robins were there!...

Today is his birthday;
So much do I care!
I came to the cemetery
And the robins were there!...

Chapter 3 | Prayers in the Loss of a Loved One

My heart was renewed!
Gone was despair!
For when I arrived,
The robins were there!

Of all the forces that make for a better world, none is so indispensable, none so powerful, as hope. Without hope, men are only half alive. With hope, they dream and think and work.
– Charles Sawyer

There is no medicine like hope, no incentive so great, and no tonic so powerful as expectation of something tomorrow.
– O. S. Marden

Tears Within My Heart | K.M. Bowman

Deuteronomy 1: 6-7, 'He said, '"When we were at Mt. Sinai, the Lord our God said to us, "You have stayed long enough at this mountain. Break camp, and move on."

Ecclesiastes 3: 1, 4, "Everything that happens in this world happens at the time God chooses. He sets the time for sorrow and the time for joy."

Changes

You were with me through the changes, Lord,
And You are with me now,
And as I face an unknown future,
My pledge to You I vow...

Five years ago I did not know
My husband I would lose,
His brother's death, my sister's death,
And that we'd have to move...

Nor that the economy would be bad,
That money would be less,
Nor that we both would be stricken with
An illness of great duress...

But You have guided step by step
Through many a trial and test,
And in the ones that are yet to come,
You'll be there as in the rest...

Chapter 3 | Prayers in the Loss of a Loved One

I place my hand in Yours, O Lord,
In faith and hope and trust,
Please guide me in uncertain paths
The way You feel You must.

Lord, when we are wrong, make us willing to change. And when we are right, make us easy to live with.
– Peter Marshall

One of the most difficult things to accept, particularly for the old, is change. Change should be seen not as accidental to life but as part of life itself.
– Hubert Van Zeller

There is nothing permanent except change.
– Heraclitus

We must adjust to changing times and still hold to unchanging principles.
– Jimmy Carter

Tears Within My Heart | K.M. Bowman

Job 32: 7, "I thought, 'Age should speak; advanced years should teach wisdom. But it is the spirit in a man, the breath of the Almighty, that gives him understanding."

Change

Change is among us, Lord,
Is with us every day,
Nothing is more certain
Than change has come to stay…

Be it job, location, or death,
Change will always be,
It's how I view the change
That binds or sets me free…

Getting beyond the boundaries
When loneliness sets in,
Reaching above myself
To grasp Your greater strength…

When confronting change,
Adapting is the key,
When suffering loss of meaning,
I must reach out to fill a need…

When losing sense of direction,
I must ask You for Your plan,
Then trust beyond a doubt
As You take me by the hand…

Chapter 3 | Prayers in the Loss of a Loved One

Your wisdom's beyond all knowledge;
Your grace more than sufficient;
Your strength beyond all weakness;
Your plan more than efficient...

It is You who allows change to come,
For it is You who are in control,
That I might learn to trust You
In the journey of my soul...

For when trust is in You alone,
And to You I'm anchored secure,
No matter what change may come,
You give perseverance to endure...

Even though I'm facing this change, Lord,
And change has come to stay,
You will give me courage
To meet the challenge of change each day.

The truth is, any major move or change in our lives can leave us disoriented and insecure. Oddly enough, however, it is in these very situations that you and I may encounter God as never before. These are the times to seek His face and His will with renewed intensity.
– Jack Hayford

Tears Within My Heart | K.M. Bowman

II Cor 1: 3-4 RSV: Blessed be the God and Father of our Lord Jesus Christ, the Father of mercies and God of all comfort, who comforts us in all our affliction, so that we may be able to comfort those who are in any affliction with the comfort with which we ourselves are comforted by God.

Comforted by God

You are comforting me, O Lord,
That I may comfort others,
Be a source of real encouragement
To my sisters and my brothers. ...

Whether in the loss of loved ones
Or in daily stress each day
You're there to give me comfort
And strength to go my way. ...

May I take that source of comfort
That comes from You alone
And pass it on to others
With the strength that I have known.

Chapter 3 | Prayers in the Loss of a Loved One

In order to console, there is no need to say much. It is enough to listen, to understand, to love.
– Paul Tournier

No matter how hard the times, no matter how sad the personal story. God's eternal comfort and joy await all who trust themselves in faith to Him.
– Douglas Stuart

To ease another's heartache is to forget one's own.
– Abraham Lincoln

Tears Within My Heart | *K.M. Bowman*

John 12: 24, "I tell you the truth, unless a kernel of wheat falls to the ground and dies, it remains only a single seed. But if it dies, it produces many seeds.

Psalm 116: 15, "Precious in the sight of the Lord is the death of His saints.

Divine Appointment

Two ladies were there
As I waited that day
For the car repair
To get under way...

They were talking and sharing
As I heard them say,
"My husband just died
And I feel lonely each day"...

So we three began talking
As if appointed by the divine
And discovered we all lost our husbands
Within a six months' time...

We were all struggling with grief
In our journeys ahead,
Feeling lonely and sad
And wondering how we'd be led...

That God meets our needs
However sad they may be
With unending love
And goodness we see...

That our unexpected meeting
In the waiting room that day
Was not by chance
But God's hand led the way...

By divine appointment
God had us to meet,
To give us all encouragement
In our trials of defeat...

That death is not the end
Of our journey here
But only the beginning
Of a journey more dear.

Chapter 3 | Prayers in the Loss of a Loved One

But we all did agree
In this suffering test,
That God's mercies are good
And He always does what is best...

Instead of separating us from others, death can unite us with others; instead of being sorrowful, it can give rise to new joy; instead of simply ending life, it can begin something new.
– Henri J. M. Nouwen

When we can face death with hope, we can live life with generosity.
– Henri J. M. Nouwen

Tears Within My Heart | *K.M. Bowman*

Rev. 21: 3, "And I heard a great voice out of heaven saying, 'Behold, the tabernacle of God is with men, and he will dwell with them, and they shall be His people and God Himself shall be with them, and be their God.'"

Going Home

What now, O Lord?
The pain is there;
It's hard to take!
It's hard to bear!...

She softly cries,
Her tears roll down
Comfort her, Lord,
With your arms around...

She's been so courageous,
So positive, so brave,
All that she had
To others she gave...

Now the cancer is winning,
Her frail body is weak
Draw her close to you, Lord,
In peace that she seeks...

Don't let her suffer,
I see pain in her face,

Chapter 3 | Prayers in the Loss of a Loved One

Just surround her with care
With your love and grace...

She's going home, Lord,
To be with you,
Just take her hand,
Guide her safely through...

And when the time comes,
Help me let her go
My sister, my friend,
I love her so...

Help me surrender her
In peace and rest,
Knowing when it comes to sisters, Lord,
You gave me the best.

I want to know one thing—the way to heaven; how to land safe on that happy shore.
– John Wesley

If you don't enter the kingdom of heaven by God's way, you cannot enter at all.
– D. L. Moody

Tears Within My Heart | K.M. Bowman

II Cor. 5: 1 WEB, "For we know that if the earthly house of our tent is dissolved, we have a building from God, a house not made with hands, eternal, in the heavens."

Going Home

Dark heavy clouds,
Like the heaviness in my heart,
My sister's nearing death
And soon the time to part

And when you call her home, Lord,
Her loving arms embrace,
Just hold her close to you
With your mercy and your grace

And I who am on earth,
Give me comfort and your peace,
Knowing now my sister's with you
And her blessings never cease.

Chapter 3 | Prayers in the Loss of a Loved One

What is heaven, but to be with God, to dwell with Him, to realize that God is mine, and I am His?
– Charles Spurgeon

Our way to heaven lies through the wilderness of this world.
– Matthew Henry

From the glimpses of heaven given us by Jesus, we know that whatever else heaven it, it is full of joy.
– Ken Gire

Tears Within My Heart | K.M. Bowman

Philippians 4: 7, "The peace of God which passes all understanding shall guard your hearts and minds in Christ Jesus."

Is It Well?

"It is well with my soul,"
The familiar words ring,
But how is it well with my soul,
When my soul cannot sing?...

Horatio G. Spafford
Lost his daughters – all four,
When they perished at sea
In the storm's fierce roar...

On a ship while at sea
Near the spot they all drowned,
Spafford penned this great hymn
Amidst pain, peace he found...

How could it be "well"
For Spafford in his grief?
He remembered where peace is found
And his soul found relief...

You give me that peace, Lord,
When to You I release grief,

Chapter 3 | Prayers in the Loss of a Loved One

An unexplainable divine calmness
In which my soul finds relief...
This peace supercedes
My ability to understand
In my most difficult circumstances
The deep pain that's at hand...

It's a guard on my heart
That helps make me whole,
And in pain I can whisper,
"It is well with my soul."

With God's peace, we can stand firm in distress, disease, destruction, and even death.
– Hank Hanegraaff

There will be no peace in any soul until it is willing to obey the voice of God.
– D. L. Moody

*Author's Note: Horatio Spafford authored the words to the beloved hymn "It is Well With My Soul"

Tears Within My Heart | K.M. Bowman

Ecclesiastes 7: 3, "Sorrow is better than laughter for by the sadness of the countenance the heart is made better."

It's Raining in My Heart

It's raining in my heart, Lord,
Like when my dad passed away,
Only now, Lord, it's my sister
Who hasn't long to stay...

Each raindrop falling down
Brings a memory one by one,
Of the times we were together,
Of the things that we have done...

The years have swiftly gone
Like the raindrops falling fast,
Making memories through each year
Making memories that will last...

But it's still raining in my heart
The burden is hard to bear
To see my sister suffer
Unable her pain to share...

Unable to hear her laugh,
Unable to see her smile,
Only her form lying still
Only to live for a while...

Chapter 3 | Prayers in the Loss of a Loved One

Yes, it's raining in my heart, Lord,
Each raindrop bears the pain,
Please let this sorrow pass
That the sun may shine again.

Facing a serious illness and the certainty of death is an humbling experience...and one that wakes us up by shattering the illusion of security and health that surrounds our modern world.
– Ken Ham

Christians are not immune to the fear of death.
– Billy Graham

Though sickness, or trouble or even death itself, should come to our house, and claim our dearest ones, still they are not lost, but only gone before.
– D. L. Moody

Tears Within My Heart | K.M. Bowman

Hebrews 12: 1 KJV, "Let us run with patience."

Let Me Run with Patience

Do you know the hardest patience, Lord?
The hardest kind to bear?
It's the patience for me to keep going
Under a heavy load of care...

It takes real strength of character
Whenever a loved one dies,
Resting in a time of grief
When my heart just cries and cries...

Or after a financial setback,
Great strength to be alone,
Not knowing Your direction, Lord,
And praying for it to be known...

But the hardest patience known,
The most difficult kind to bear,
Is the power to keep on working
Under a heavy load of care...

The power to continue working
Whenever a setback comes;
The power to perform daily tasks
When grief my heart overruns...

Chapter 3 | Prayers in the Loss of a Loved One

The power to perform active service
During social events, shopping, or work place,
Contributing to other people's joy
In spite of deep sorrow I face...

So I ask not, Lord, from the clouds a rainbow
In my service to You each day,
But may I in my cloud be a rainbow
Sharing the ministry of joy on my way...

For though the patience of "running" is hard,
Continuing to work when I am sad,
I find that my heartache is healed
In my ministry to make others glad.

Have patience with all things, but chiefly have patience with yourself. Do not lose courage in considering your imperfections, but instantly set about remedying them—every day begin the task anew.
– St. Frances de Sales

Tears Within My Heart | *K.M. Bowman*

II Timothy 4: 6-8, "For I am ready to be offered, and the time of my departure is at hand. I have fought the good fight, I have finished my course. I have kept the faith: henceforth, there is laid up for me a crown of righteousness."

John 11: 25, "Jesus said to her, 'I am the resurrection and the life. He who believes in me will live, even though he dies; and whoever lives and believes in me will never die. Do you believe this?'"

Life and Immortality

Life and immortality,
Is Your gift, Lord, to me
When I believe in Your word,
And have a faith that can see...

Consider the butterfly–
With an egg its life starts,
Then hatches into larva
That grows as life's part...

Into a resting stage it goes,
Where it quietly waits
For Your design and timing,
A new creature to create...

It struggles out of the cocoon,
Looking different than before,

Chapter 3 | Prayers in the Loss of a Loved One

No longer to crawl,
It can rise and soar...

Life and death are like that,
When I die in You, Lord,
I am given a new body,
Immortality is my reward...

Life and immortality,
Your gift, Lord, to me,
When I believe in Your word
And have eyes to see.

Surely God would not have created such a being as man...to exist only for a day! No, no, man was made for immortality.
– Abraham Lincoln

Life is real, life is earnest; and the grave is not the goal; dust thou art and to dust returnest was not spoken of the soul.
– Henry Wadsworth Longfellow

Tears Within My Heart | *K.M. Bowman*

Psalm 49: 20, "A man's greatness cannot keep him from death; he will still die like the animals.

Nehemiah 8: 10, "Do not grieve, for the joy of the Lord is your strength.

Lord, Here I Am Again

Lord, here I am again,
Another friend has died,
The deaths come much too quickly now,
Please help this pain inside...

I miss her, Lord, my heart is sad,
I learned the news today,
For forty-three years we've been good friends,
Please help me now, I pray...

Sometimes it's hard to keep on going,
Though I know she's there with You,
Just pick me up and give me strength,
This sad time to go through.

Chapter 3 | Prayers in the Loss of a Loved One

Our sufferings may be hard to bear, but they teach us lessons which, in turn, equip and enable us to help others.
– Billy Graham

Out of suffering have emerged the strongest souls; the most massive characters are seared with scars.
– E. H. Chapin

Tears Within My Heart | K.M. Bowman

Ecclesiastes 3: 1-2, *"Everything that happens in this world happens at the time God chooses. He sets the time for birth and the time for death."*

My Sister's Time to Die

It was really, really hard, Lord,
The doctor's words to hear
That my sister's time to die
Is now so very near...

She is in a lot of pain
And her eyes are closed in sleep
But she knows me when I talk
And tries a smile to keep...

She's been so strong and brave,
An example for everyone
Of your mercy, love, and goodness, Lord,
And of Jesus, your only Son.

But I'll miss my only sister,
I want to share with her each day
As we did when we were children
When at work and when at play...

I love her very much
And will miss her when she's gone
Without my husband and my sister,
I wonder how I'll carry on...

Chapter 3 | Prayers in the Loss of a Loved One

I'll carry on with you, Lord,
As you give me strength to bear
My sorrow and my trials
And with you my sufferings share.

Everything science has taught me—and continues to teach me—strengthens my belief in the continuity of our spiritual existence after death. Nothing disappears without a trace.
– Wernher Von Braun

Tears Within My Heart | *K.M. Bowman*

John 6: 47-48, "Most assuredly, I say to you, he who believes in Me has everlasting life. I am the bread of life."

My Sister's Gone

My sister's gone, Lord,
Her journey on earth is done,
She is now there with you,
Her journey a brave courageous one

The time we spent together,
It seemed to go so fast,
I'll miss her Lord, I'll miss her,
But with you she is at last

No more suffering, no more pain,
She's whole again once more,
And waits to greet us one by one
With a welcome at heaven's door.

Chapter 3 | Prayers in the Loss of a Loved One

I'd like to think when life is done that I had filled a needed post, that here and there I'd paid my fare with more than idle talk and boast; that I had taken gifts divine, the breath of life and manhood fine, and tried to use them now and then in service for my fellow men.
– Edgar A. Guest

Tears Within My Heart | K.M. Bowman

Ecclesiastes 3: 1, 2b, "Everything that happens in this world happens at the time God chooses. He sets the time for planting and the time for pulling up."

Once Again It's Spring

The cattle are in the field,
The hills are turning green,
The mountain is standing tall,
And once again it's spring...

The flowers are blooming bright,
The birds in chorus sing,
The trees are budding new,
And once again it's spring...

Red buds are in bloom
With signs the season brings,
And I miss him more than ever, Lord,
When once again it's spring.

Chapter 3 | Prayers in the Loss of a Loved One

Each time I rest from daily chores and look and listen at the great outdoors, I think what a wondrous world and fair and I know that God is always there.
– Sylvia Schooler Brandt

The beauty of spring, it seems to me is the Glory of Heaven descended, as I breathe the fragrance in the air of lilacs and roses blended.
– Author Unknown

Tears Within My Heart | K.M. Bowman

John 16: 22 WEB, "Therefore you now have sorrow, but I will see you again and your heart will rejoice, and no one will take your joy away from you."

The Rainbow

Help me, O Lord, through my tears
To see the rainbow ahead,
Through the depth of the pain I feel,
By Your hand let me know I am led...

For though my vision is dimmed
By the blur of tears in my eyes,
I see your rainbow of hope
In the midst of my heart's deepest cries...

When I see Your rainbow of color,
It changes my black and my gray
To sunshine of a million tomorrows
When blessings You'll shower my way.

Chapter 3 | Prayers in the Loss of a Loved One

The soul would have no rainbow had the eye no tears.
– John Vance Chency

Those whom God uses most effectively have been hammered, filed, and tempered in the furnace of trials and heartache.
– Charles Swindoll

I John 5: 13 NKJV, "*These things I have written to you who believe in the name of the Son of God, that you may know that you have eternal life, and that you may continue to believe in the name of the Son of God.*"

The Time Has Finally Come

The time has finally come, Lord
My sister's there with you,
Her earthly journey finished,
Her eternal home in view...

No more to hear her laugh,
No more to see her smile,
No more to hear her talk,
No more to face a trial....

She was valiant and victorious
Her faith was radiant and bright
And until the very end
She fought a courageous fight....

Her life became a witness
To all who came to see
Your likeness in her living
And how you want us to be....

No more will she have to suffer,
No more pain for her to bear
Only peace and love forever
And forever in your care...

Chapter 3 | Prayers in the Loss of a Loved One

And for us left here on earth, Lord,
Give us your journey plan,
For the sorrow's running deep
And it's hard to start again....

But we'll wait for your own timing,
To take us by the hand
And lead us with assurance
On the road that you have planned.

The Lord is consistently gentle with us. He stands beside us in the midst of trouble and tragedy, nursing us through it all. This is the same kind of encouragement the people around us need.
– Lloyd John Ogilvie

And then one day He spoke to me, and, oh, I love Him so. My destiny is in His hands; he's everywhere I go.
– Dee Gaskin

> *"No discipline seems pleasant at the time, but painful. Later on, however, it produces a harvest of righteousness and peace for those who have been trained by it."*
> *– Hebrews 12:11*

"As far as the Lord is concerned, the time to stand is in the darkest moment. It is when everything seems hopeless, when there appears no way out, when God alone can deliver."

– David Wiekerron

Prayers for Deliverance

Chapter 4

Ecclesiastes 3: 1-2, "Everything that happens in this world happens at the time God chooses: a time to be born and a time to die."

A Touch of Sadness and A Promise

They were there that early spring day,
Blowing in the wind,
Dead and dried oak leaves,
Their life had come to an end...

But what a promise where they lay
Of all that is yet to be,
For there was a bed of crocus blooms
For all the world to see...

Hundreds of golden blooms
Covered the brown leaf ground,
A promise of brand new life
In the midst of the old could be found...

I feel like those old dried leaves, Lord,
Growing older every day,
But You bring me Your touch of renewal,
And bright promise You're with me to stay...

Chapter 4 | Prayers for Deliverance

A time to be born and grow,
A time to grow old and die,
You know the perfect timing, Lord,
For "a touch of sadness and a promised reply."

Birth is the beginning of death.
– Thomas Fuller

Every man must do two things alone: he must do his own believing and his own dying.
– Martin Luther

Romans 8: 28-29: "And we know that all things work together for good to them that love God, to them who are called according to His purpose. For I am persuaded, that neither death, nor life, not angels, nor things to come, nor height, nor depth, nor any creature, shall be able to separate us from the love of God which is in Christ Jesus, our Lord."

Adversities or Opportunities?

Adversities or opportunities, Lord?
A time to triumph or a time to give in?
A time to be depressed?
Or a time to praise You within?...

For nothing can separate me from Your love–
Not things present nor things to come,
Not principalities, nor powers,
Nor life, nor death, no, not one...

Hope is not based on circumstance;
Hope is based on You alone,
By learning to trust You in adversity
And letting Your power be shown...

Adversities or opportunities, Lord?
A time for my faith to grow;
A time for deeper trust to know;
A time for greater witness to show.

Chapter 4 | Prayers for Deliverance

Adversity in the things of this world opens the door for spiritual salvation.
– A. J. Toynbee

Comfort and prosperity have never enriched the world as much as adversity has.
– Billy Graham

II Tim. 4: 7, "I have fought the good fight; I have finished the race; I have kept the faith."

Finishers

Are you a finisher for the Lord?
Do you stop what you begin?
Or do you work on diligently
Until you're at the end?

Paul was a finisher
In his ministry for the Lord,
He had no unfinished business
As he went to his final reward...

In these words are his final farewell,
"I have kept the faith;
I have fought the good fight;
I have finished the race." (II Timothy 4: 7)

Can I, like Paul, run my race, Lord,
With eternity in view?
Can I also be a finisher
Of what You give me to do?

Let me run my race
With perseverance in mind
That my reward might be
Of the eternal kind.

Chapter 4 | Prayers for Deliverance

Perseverance is a great element of success. If you only knock long enough and loud enough at the gates, you are sure to wake up somebody.
– Henry Wadsworth Longfellow

Hebrews 12: 6 (NIV), "The Lord disciplines those He loves."

Revelations 3: 19 (AMP), "Those whom I dearly and tenderly love...I tell their faults...convict and convince...reprove and chasten."

Hebrews 12:7-11 (NLT), "No discipline is enjoyable while it is happening-it is painful! But afterward, there will be a peaceful harvest of right living for those who are trained in this way."

God's Discipline

"The Lord disciplines all those that He loves,"
Am I being disciplined, Lord, today?
May I be patient in the discipline of Your hand
And You will show me the way...

How is it that You discipline me, Lord?
You tell me when I'm out of line,
You convict, convince, reprove, and chasten
With Your careful discipline divine...

Why is it that You discipline me?
That in Your holiness I might share–
That I might live in Your kingdom forever
To enjoy Your love and Your care.

Chapter 4 | Prayers for Deliverance

No discipline is enjoyable while it is happening,
It is painful for me to bear,
But afterward I'll experience the peace of right living
When trained in this way of Your care.

The greatest firmness is the greatest mercy.
– Henry Wadsworth Longfellow

Make us masters of ourselves that we may be the servants of others.
– Sir Alexander Paterson

Self-discipline never means giving up anything–for giving up is a loss. Our Lord did not ask us to give up the things of earth, but to exchange them for better things.
– Fulton J. Sheen

Tears Within My Heart | *K.M. Bowman*

Psalm 23: 6, "I know that your goodness and love will be with me all my life; and your house will be my home as long as I live."

God's Love

Timeless as the mountains, Lord,
Endless as the sea,
Ageless as the deep blue sky
Is Your love for me...

Joyful as the flowers that bloom,
Happy as birds that sing,
Cheerful as a smile that's bright
Is the love to me You bring...

Trusting, Lord, let me look to You,
Faithful in how I live,
Sharing the love You give to me
Among those with whom I live.

Chapter 4 | Prayers for Deliverance

If you have love in your life, it can make up for a great many things you lack. If you don't have it, no matter what else there is, it's not enough.
– Sir James M. Barrie

Our Lord does not care so much for the importance of our works as for the love with which they are done.
– St. Teresa of Avila

So often when we say "I love you," we say it with a huge "I" and a small "you."
– Antony, Russian Orthodox Archbishop

Tears Within My Heart | K.M. Bowman

John 3:16, "For God so loved the world that He gave His only begotten Son that whosoever believeth in Him should not perish but have everlasting life."

God's Love Endless as the Ocean

I stood on deck and looked around
As far as I could see–
The restless sea and rolling waves
Stretched to infinity...

Only You and me, O Lord,
And the bright blue sky above,
The wisps of clouds wrapping ever 'round,
Like the arms of Your great love...

As endless as the ocean, Lord,
As deep as depths unknown,
Is Your great love for all of us
Touching hearts of coldest stone.

Chapter 4 | Prayers for Deliverance

God loves each of us as if there were only one of us.
– Augustine

The love of God is one of the great realities of the universe, a pillar upon which the hope of the world rests. But it is a personal, intimate thing, too. God does not love populations. He loves people. He loves not masses, but men.
– A. W. Tozer

Luke 6: 36, "Be merciful just as your Father is merciful."

Galatians 6: 9-10 (NIV), "Let us not become weary in doing good, for at the proper time, we will reap a harvest if we do not give up. Therefore, as we have opportunity, let us do good to all people."

Ephesians 2: 8 (NIV), "By grace you have been saved through faith—and this not from yourselves, it is the gift of God."

Grace

It was in the parking garage
When damaged beyond repair,
He could have been angry at the unknown lady
Who ran into his new car there...

Instead, he asked her
If she was OK,
Then she began to cry
As she shared that day...

"My doctor just told me I have terminal cancer,
That plans must now be made;
I'm worried about my precious family,
I feel so lost and afraid"...

Chapter 4 | Prayers for Deliverance

Instead of the anger
He first felt in his heart,
He prayed with her asking
God to do His part...

GRACE is what it's all about, Lord,
In my earthly encounters each day–
The aggressive co-worker, annoying neighbor,
Family member who wants his own way...

The mercy and grace You give to me
Can transform me to give to others,
For the grace I receive is the grace I can give
To all of my sisters and brothers.

Man is born broken, he lives by mending. The Grace of God is the glue.
– Eugene O'Neill

The word grace emphasizes at one and the same time the helpless poverty of man and the limitless kindness of God.
– William Barclay

Tears Within My Heart | K.M. Bowman

Romans 8: 38-39, "I am persuaded that nothing shall be able to separate us from the love of God which is in Christ Jesus, our Lord."

Immeasurable Is God's Love

Inexhaustible is Your mercy, Lord,
Immeasurable is Your grace,
Inexpressible is Your peace,
Indefinable are Your ways...

Boundless is Your righteousness,
Infinite is Your love,
Endless is Your compassion,
Generous Your giving from above...

Unparalleled is Your excellence,
Unmatched is Your power,
Unimaginable Your majesty,
Unequaled strength in life's darkest hour...

Inexpressible is the joy,
Immeasurable in my heart,
As I give You glory and honor
For the love that You impart.

Chapter 4 | Prayers for Deliverance

I have lived a long time, sir, and the longer I live, the more convincing proofs I see of this truth—that God governs in the affairs of men.
– Benjamin Franklin

The truth about man is that he needs to be loved the most when he deserves it the least. Only God can fulfill this incredible need. Only God can provide a love so deep it saves from the depths.
– Anonymous

Tears Within My Heart | *K.M. Bowman*

Psalm 119: 71, "My punishment was good for me, because it made me learn Your commands."

Job 23: 10-11, "Yet God knows every step I take; if he tests me, he will find me pure. I follow faithfully the road He chooses, and never wander to either side."

II Cor. 12: 9-10, "But his answer was: 'My grace is all you need, for my power is strongest when you are weak.' I am most happy, then to be proud of my weaknesses, in order to feel the protection of Christ's power over me. I am content with weaknesses, insults, hardships, persecutions, and difficulties for Christ's sake. For when I am weak, then I am strong."

In Your Hands Are Strength and Power

Wealth and honor come from You, O Lord,
You are the ruler of all things,
In Your hands are strength and power,
In You my heart sings...

I will speak now of my weaknesses,
So Your power may rest on me,
In my weaknesses, hardships, and difficulties,
The power of Your strength I see...

You have led me all these years, O Lord,

Chapter 4 | Prayers for Deliverance

And have humbled me with many tests
To know what was in my heart
And how I would serve You best...

In Your steps, Lord, my feet have followed,
Without turning aside, I have kept to Your way,
And with Your strength will I still follow You
Throughout the rest of my days...

You have taught me obedience, Lord,
For You are the ruler of all things,
In Your hands are strength and power,
In You always my heart sings.

I can see how it might be possible for a man to look down upon the earth and be an atheist, but I cannot conceive how he could look up into the heavens and say there is no God.
– Abraham Lincoln

How Thou canst think so well of us, And be the God Thou art, Is darkness to my intellect, But sunshine to my heart.
– Anonymous

Tears Within My Heart | K.M. Bowman

Genesis 32: 24, "So Jacob was left alone and a man wrestled with him till daybreak."

Psalm 104: 34, "May my meditation be pleasing to Him, as I rejoice in the Lord."

Left Alone!

Left alone, Lord,
In the quiet and still,
Your voice to hear,
Your presence to feel...

Left alone!
You make no mistakes
In my time alone
That You want to take...

Left alone!
To be restored and renewed,
To continue the work, Lord,
For You to do...

Yes, left alone!
With You in prayer
That others see in my life
Your presence there.

Chapter 4 | Prayers for Deliverance

The mightiest works of God are the fruit of silence.
– F. B. Meyer

The word of God penetrates through the thick of human verbosity to the silent center of our heart; silence opens in us the space where the word can be heard.
– Henri J. M. Nouwen

> *"Marvel not what I said unto thee, ye must be born again."*
> *John 3:7*

"We have no reason to expect pardon, except we seek it by faith in Christ and that is always attended by the repentance, and followed by newness of life, by hatred of sin, and love to God."
– Matthew Henry

Prayers for Restoration

Chapter 5

Tears Within My Heart | K.M. Bowman

Joel 2: 25, KJV, "I will restore to you the years the locust hath eaten."

My Life Is Now in Ruin, Lord

My life in now in ruin, Lord,
I am broken in despair,
No one understands!
No one seems to care!

Peter felt that way, too,
After Jesus he denied;,
He wept long and bitterly;
He went outside and cried!...

He was close to Jesus;
One of His intimate friends,
In everything, they shared–
To the crucifixion end...

That's when Peter failed,
When asked to risk his life,
When three times he denied
    the Lord
In the crucifixion strife...
    (Matt. 26: 69-75)

That's when You stepped in–
You specialize in restoration;
Your specialty is broken
    hearts--

To mend them in
    preparation...

For a ministry great and wide
That otherwise could not be
Where broken hearts are
    used
To draw others on bended
    knee...

Peter was given a chance
To reaffirm his love
And became the Pentecost
    keynote speaker
With Your power from
above...

I feel my life is ruined, Lord,
In brokenness and despair,
I bring to you my pieces–
For Your specialty is repair...

You will take the many
    fragments
And pieces of my soul,

Chapter 5 | Prayers for Restoration

And with mercy and forgiveness
Make them beautiful and whole...

You will use my past mistakes
To give me a ministry of my own
Reflecting Your likeness in me
In amazing ways unknown...

Till others are drawn to You, Lord,
By my word and by my deed
And my greatest work for You
Will be to meet Your greatest need.

As I come before You now, O Lord,
My life in ruin lies,
Please take my fragmented pieces,
And a new life now devise.

No storm is so great, no wave is so high, no sea is so deep, no wind is so strong, that Jesus cannot either calm it or carry us through it.
– Anne Graham Lotz

God promises us forgiveness for what we have but we need His deliverance from what we are.
– Corrie ten Boom

God's rescue plan—to be delivered, you have to let go.
– Sheila Walsh

Tears Within My Heart | *K.M. Bowman*

Jeremiah 31: 3, "Yea, I have loved thee with an everlasting love; therefore, with loving kindness have I drawn thee."

It Was Love

It was love that let the prophets speak–
Love–their prophecy fulfilled;
It was love that gave compassion to the weak,
Love was His Father's will;
It was love that restrained Him when falsely accused,
Love that forgave the thief;
It was love that made Him the torture refuse,
Love that brought disbelief;
It was love that led way despising the shame,
Love that said, "Father, forgive!"
It was in love I remember Your holy name,
Your love, Lord, showed me how I should live.

Chapter 5 | Prayers for Restoration

We must die to ourselves as we minister in love to others. If the giving gets tough, we can look up to Him and say, "He did it; in His strength, so can I."
– Margaret Johnston Hess

And love in the heart wasn't put there to stay; love isn't love till you give it away.
– Oscar Hammerstein II

The love of our neighbor is the only door out of the dungeon of self.
– George MacDonald

Tears Within My Heart | *K.M. Bowman*

Job 14: 1, 4, "Man that is born of a woman is of few days...His days are determined, the number of his months are with thee, thou has appointed his bounds that he cannot pass."

Life Is Like a Shadow

Life is like a shadow, Lord,
Like a fleeting, floating cloud,
Like a willowy wisp of smoke,
Like a sound that's soft, then loud...

For every single one of us,
Time is slowly, slipping away,
And every day we wonder,
"Will we go or will we stay?"...

If I am prepared to die, O Lord,
Then I am also prepared to live,
What's important in my journey
Is how much love each day I give.

Chapter 5 | Prayers for Restoration

This is the way to live – that after you are gone, people will wish that you were still around to give them comfort and counsel, love and care, understanding and concern.
– Louis Benes

Your life is like a coin. You can spend it any way you wish, but you can spend it only once.
– Lillian Dickson

Life is short. Plans for each day should be lived in the realization that it is God who will decide if we shall live. Our decision is whether or not to do His will.
– Donald A. Miller

Tears Within My Heart | K.M. Bowman

Psalm 93: 4 NRSV, "More majestic than the thunders of mighty waters, more majestic than the waves of the sea, majestic on high is the Lord!"

Limitless Is Your Love, O Lord

More majestic than the thunders of mighty waters,
More majestic than the waves of the sea,
More majestic than the peaks of towering grandeur,
Is Your love, O Lord, for me...

Limitless, O Lord, Your power to forgive,
Limitless Your compassionate heart,
Limitless Your power of healing
In a world that's torn apart...

Unfathomable mercy You give, O Lord,
Unfathomable grace to receive,
Unfathomable blessings You give
To all who are faithful and believe.

Chapter 5 | Prayers for Restoration

A man can no more diminish God's glory by refusing to worship Him than a lunatic can put out the sun by scribbling the word "darkness" on the walls of his cell.
C. S. Lewis

Fulfillment in life comes not by the love of power, but by the power of love.
– Anonymous

Love has hands to help others. It has feet to hasten to the poor and needy. It has eyes to see misery and want. It has ears to hear the sighs and sorrows of men. This is what love looks like.
-Augustine

Tears Within My Heart | K.M. Bowman

-Isaiah 43: 19, "Behold, I will do something new, now it will spring forth; will you not be aware of it? I will even make a roadway in the wilderness, rivers in the desert."

New Beginnings

You are a God of New Beginnings, Lord,
You who made the earth,
Hung it on a spindle,
And gave it grace and worth...

You are a God of New Beginnings
In our lives as well,
Marriage, new home, a baby,
Milestones that in time will tell...

You are all about newness, Lord,
In the covenant with us You made,
That each time we take communion,
The old things have passed away.

Please do a new thing in my life, Lord,
Like making a river in my desert dry,
Like making a roadway in my wilderness difficult,
Like making a bridge over my sorrow wide...

I am in a desert place, O Lord,
Everything seems dried up and old,
Only You have the key to New Beginnings,
Only You can let them unfold...

Chapter 5 | Prayers for Restoration

Take my regret, my shame, my sins, and mistakes,
The things to which I am bound,
Break those chains with new vision and purpose,
For only in You, can new life be found.

Our gifts and attainments are not only to be light and warmth in our own dwellings, but are also to shine through the windows into the dark night, to guide and cheer bewildered travelers on the road.
– Henry Ward Beecher

Stay focused on God's ways and principles. Live every day in the knowledge that He loves you and He is present within you, enabling you to do mighty things for His kingdom.
– George Barna

For all those dark times, here's a word of hope: God meets us where we are. Even if we aren't looking in His direction, He is always looking in ours.
– Liz Curtis Higgs

Tears Within My Heart | K.M. Bowman

Philippians 3: 8 NIV, "I consider everything a loss compared to the surpassing greatness of knowing Christ."

Only God Fills the Empty Place

I seem to race, Lord, from one thing to another,
Driven by accomplishment, I fail to see my brother,
Lasting fulfillment doesn't come in just reaching another goal,
But in Your eyes it's realizing the worth of my soul,
I ask myself, "Why am I doing what I do? Who am I doing it for?"
My answers will be revealing in the priorities I store,
For I can only fulfill Your purpose, Lord, by building a relationship with You
For my energy will grow weak unless You restore and renew,
Another credential won't do it; nor another trophy to win;
Not another award to receive; nor even the praise of men...
Only You can restore what my striving has depleted;
Only You can complete what my life needs to be completed;
In Your presence, crowns lose their luster and grow dim
And meaningless are the empty accolades in the praise of men;
Only You can fill that deep empty place!
Everything else is a loss compared to Your mercy and grace!

Chapter 5 | Prayers for Restoration

A central message of the Bible is that we can only have a relationship with God by sheer grace. Our moral efforts are too feeble and falsely motivated to ever merit salvation.
– Timothy Keller

God's grace does not come to people who morally outperform others, but to those who admit their failure to perform and who acknowledge their need for a Savior.
– Timothy Keller

God's grace is just that–grace, unmerited favor. Nothing I will do can ever cause Him to love me more or less.
– David Hawkins

Revelation 5: 13 WEB, "I heard every created thing which is in heaven, on the earth, under the earth, on the sea, and everything in them, saying, 'To Him who sits on the throne, and to the Lamb be the blessing, the honor, the glory, and the dominion, forever and ever! Amen.'"

Psalm 62: 5-6 WEB, "My soul, wait in silence for God alone, for my expectation is from Him. He alone is my rock and my salvation, my fortress. I will not be shaken."

My Sacred Place

Where do you go for your sacred place
To be with God alone?
To really pour your heart to God
That to you He might be known?

I go to a place called Capital Reef,
A beautiful place in the West,
Where time stands still and my spirit's filled
With creation among God's best...

Here it's as if the earth just began
With canyons and cliffs and such
And standing in awe of this majestic place,
I can feel God's powerful touch...

Chapter 5 | Prayers for Restoration

Or in the darkness of night with the moon shining bright
And the canyon walls' soft radiant glow,
God's hand is upon me, His presence surrounds me,
As nearer His heart I grow...

I also go to Antelope Canyon
In the Arizona desert near Page,
An enchanted canyon carved by wind and water
In the midst of the sand and the sage...

Upon entering this place the walls glow inside,
And the shapes no words can describe,
The sun shines through giving an ethereal view
Of God as my heavenly guide...

But we don't have to go to far away places
Or cross over boundless seas,
Our sacred place can be right where we are
In God's presence on bended knees.

True holiness is learning to enjoy friendship with God.
– M. P. Horban

II Corinthians 3: 5, "Our sufficiency is from God."

Philippians 4: 13, "I can do all things through Christ who strengthens me."

Our Sufficiency Is from God

My sufficiency is from You, Lord,
It is You who care;
When I am feeling inadequate,
You are there!...

It requires Your involvement,
When You give an assignment to do,
Working <u>with</u> You not <u>for</u> You
Ensures success to get through...

I think of Moses instructing Pharoah
To let his work force leave
To go worship a God
In whom he didn't believe...

I think of Jonah going to Nineveh,
Most corrupt city You, our Lord, to defy,
When he preached to the people,
"Repent or die!"

Chapter 5 | Prayers for Restoration

Or I think of Jeremiah's message,
A hard-hearted people to reach,
He cried because they refused to listen,
You strengthened him in his call to preach...

When You called Your servants,
They didn't just jump up and say,
"No problem! I can handle that!
I will begin today!"

They felt inadequate
In their work called to do
Till they surrendered to You
And let You carry through...

When I don't have the finances,
You give me all I need,
When I don't have the ability,
You equip me as You intercede....

When I don't have strength,
You make me strong when I'm weak,
You are involved in my assignment,
When it's You I seek.

What God expects us to attempt, He enables us to achieve.
– Stephen Olford

Tears Within My Heart | K.M. Bowman

Revelation 2: 10, "Be thou fruitful unto death and I will give thee a crown of life."

Swifter Than A Weaver's Shuttle

Swifter, Lord, than a weaver's shuttle
Is my life on earth each day;
It is like a vapor here for awhile,
Then it quickly vanishes away...

What is my life? What does it say?
In the face of eternity?
It is a flower that fades, grass that withers,
A sunset stretching endlessly...

Swiftly move the shuttles,
Swift as the speed of light,
How am I living each of my days?
For You, Lord, or the darkness of night?

Chapter 5 | Prayers for Restoration

As soon as man is born, he begins to die.
– Unknown

It matters not how a man dies, but how he lives. The act of dying is not of importance, it lasts so short a time.
– Samuel Johnson

Tears Within My Heart | *K.M. Bowman*

John 15: 2, "Every branch that does bear fruit he prunes so that it will be even more fruitful."

The Trials You Give, Lord

I do not question, Lord,
The trials You give,
For the trials You send
Are to help me live...

When a gardener stops pruning
And trimming his trees,
He knows the season of bearing
Has finished and ceased...

He leaves it alone
Because its fruitfulness is done,
And any further effort
Would help it yield none...

Now I understand, Lord,
Why you lead as You do,
Freedom from suffering
Means I'm no use to you...

I can only serve greatly
When You prune with Your knife,
Giving me larger growth
And a fuller life...

Chapter 5 | Prayers for Restoration

Knowing the little fruit
I produce for You now,
Will increase in abundance
As You trim each bough...

So don't leave me alone, Lord,
But with Your tenderest touch,
Prune and cut and trim
That I now will bear much.

The gem cannot be polished without friction, nor man perfected without trials.
– Unknown

God has a meaning in each blow of His chisel, each incision of His knife. He knows the way that He takes.
– F. B. Meyer

> *"If any of you lack wisdom, let him ask of God, that giveth to all men liberally and upbraideth not; and it shall be given him." – James 1:5*

"Be guided, only by the healer of the sick, the raiser of the dead, the friend of all who were afflicted and forlorn, the patient Master who shed tears of compassion for our infirmities. We cannot but be right when we put the rest away, and do everything in remembrance of Him... There can be no confusion in following Him, and seeking for no other footsteps. I am certain!"
– Charles Dickens

Prayers When I need God's Guidance

Chapter 6

Tears Within My Heart | K.M. Bowman

Genesis 45: 8 NIV, "It was not you who sent me here, but God."

"But God" Moments

Sometimes I have a "but God" moment, Lord,
In my journey here on earth,
I struggle for Your direction
To discover my self worth…

Before I trust You completely,
I want You Your plan to reveal,
Am I willing to step out in faith
To fully follow Your will?

You don't give the whole picture, Lord,
For impossible it may appear,
I may become overwhelmed
With so many obstacles near…

But one thing I know for certain,
One thing has its appeal,
I need You to lead and guide me
Your mission to fulfill…

Take Joseph who was sent to Egypt,
His brothers sold him out,
"But God" used it to preserve
The Jewish race–without a doubt…

The Israelites were in slavery,

Chapter 6 | Prayers When I need God's Guidance

In a dark and weary land,
"But God" sent Moses to lead them
To the hope-filled Promised Land...

Jesus died on the cross
And His death seemed so in vain,
"But God" used his death to save us
And give the world a greater gain...

Yes, there are "but God" moments in my life
When I've reached the end of my rope,
Then I've felt Your hand upon me, Lord,
Divinely helping me cope...

You can take my circumstances, Lord,
And create moments divine,
When I say, "'But God' used them to show me
He's leading me all the time..."

It is You, Lord, who are in control,
You know for me what is best,
With Your divine "But God" moments,
You'll help me endure the tests.

God does not will every circumstance; but He does have a will in every circumstance.
– J. Kenneth Grider

If God's will is your will and if He always has His way with you, then you always have your way also.
– Hannah Whitall Smith

Acts 7: 30, 33-34, "after 40 years had passed, an angel appeared to Moses...in the desert...Then the Lord said to him, '...Now come, I will send you back to Egypt.'"

Ecclesiastes 3: 7, "A time to rend, and a time to sew; a time to keep silence, and a time to speak..."

Called to Be Still

Am I being called aside now, Lord, for a time to be still
Before You ask me another mission to fill?
Then may I peacefully wait till the next step will be
And when You're ready Your work You'll call me to see,
And while I am waiting, let my hope not grow faint
For I know You will guide me when I make no complaint,
Quite often You ask me to wait before I go
To recover from my last mission and my next step to know,
So whenever You call, Lord, on a mission to be,
I'll place my hand in Yours that Your work I might see.

Chapter 6 | Prayers When I need God's Guidance

Solitude and silence are not, in the end, about success and failure. They are about showing up and letting God do the rest. They are not an end in themselves; they are merely a means through which we regularly make ourselves available to God for the intimacy of relationship and for the work of transformation that only God can accomplish.
– Ruth Haley Barton

We do the praying, but not the waiting. Let us not be afraid to be silent before Him thinking it is wasted time.
– John Wright Follette

Mark 7:33 "He took him aside, away from the crowd."

Lamentations 3: 26, "It is good that a man should both hope and quietly wait for the salvation of the Lord."

Being Still

You have called me to be still, Lord, called me aside for awhile,
In the midst of life's busy pace,
To be a caregiver for my husband's illness,
Which has slowed me in the midst of the race…

Help me rise above it all, Lord, and look up to You
To see only the work of Your hand
That from my place of bondage will come encouraging ministry
That only You could have planned. …

I think of John Bunyan, imprisoned 12 years
And the book he was inspired to write
Except the Bible, read more than any other book
To weary pilgrims it brought hope and light

And how did Paul handle the darkness of prison?
With triumphant songs of praise,
With letters to churches and witnessing to soldiers,
He was victorious in those dark prison days

And Madam Guyon, the sweet-spirited French saint,
Endured time behind prison walls,
The music of her soul has traveled far beyond
To encourage the hearts of us all…

Chapter 6 | Prayers When I need God's Guidance

You have called me to be still, Lord, called me aside for awhile
In the midst of life's busy pace,
You are calling me now for Your special mission
For only this time and this place.

From these moments of quietness let light go forth, and joy, and power, that will remain with me through all the hours of the day.
– John Baillie

Quiet is a blessed gift. In this frantic world, how we must cherish every moment of it, and carve it out for ourselves every moment we get.
– Anne Ortlund

Genesis 18: 14, "Is anything too hard for the Lord?"

Genesis 37: 9 (KJV), "He dreamed still another dream."

Dream Your Dream

Let me dream my dream! Set my goals!
Keep my dream alive!
And You in Your wisdom will work with me, Lord,
My dream to realize…

"But the challenge looks far too big for me!"
I sometimes want to say,
But nothing is too big for You, O Lord,
Nothing can stand in Your way…

I can never out-dream Your infinite plans,
"Is anything too hard for the Lord?" (Genesis 18: 14)
Let me dream my dream! Set my goals!
And great will be my reward!

Chapter 6 | Prayers When I need God's Guidance

If you don't know where you are going, every road will get you nowhere.
– Henry Kissinger

It must be borne in mind that the tragedy of life doesn't lie in not reaching your goal. The tragedy lies in having no goal to reach.
– Benjamin E. Mays

If one advances confidently in the direction of his dreams, and endeavors to live the life which he has imagined, he will meet with a success unexpected in common hours.
– Henry David Thoreau

If you can dream it, you can do it. It's all about possibilities. You can go anywhere from nowhere.
– Robert Schuller

Tears Within My Heart | K.M. Bowman

Matt. 6: 28: "See how the lilies of the field grow."

God Knows Best

Once a man planted a tree,
"Lord, my tree needs rain," he prayed,
And the Lord sent gentle showers
To help the tree He made…

Then the man prayed,
"Lord, my tree needs sun,"
And the Lord sent warming sunshine
To help the work that was begun…

"Now send frost, dear Lord,
To strengthen the roots that abide,"
And the Lord sent sparkling frost,
But by evening, the tree had died…

The man lamented to his friend
Of the strange experience he shared,
How his little tree had died
With all of his loving care…

His friend thoughtfully said,
"I, too, planted a tree,
But I entrust it now to God
Who knows best what it needs…

Chapter 6 | Prayers When I need God's Guidance

"For He who has made it
Knows just what to send–
Rain, sun, or frost,
For its growth to extend...

"I gave God no conditions
Except only to pray–
You know what it needs, Lord,
Please send it today."

So whatever my concern, Lord,
If I seek it in prayer,
You will meet my needs
And my burden will bear...

You are in control;
You know every test;
You care for my needs
And will send what is best.

God has a thousand ways, where I can see not one; when all my means have reached their end, then His have just begun.
– Esther Guyot

John 11: 40, "Did I not tell you that if you believed, you would see the glory of God?"

Romans 8: 28, "And we know that in all things God works for the good of those who love Him, who have been called according to His purpose."

God Knows Best

You know best, Lord,
When twists and turns my life may take,
You know best the way to lead
When I face my each mistake…

You know best
When sadness and sorrow take their place,
You know just what I'm feeling
As You give me Your comfort and grace…

You know best
When joy and happiness my family shares,
When Your blessings inspire me
And I know gladness beyond compare…

You know best
In all things I face each day;
You know best how to hold the reins
And guide me along life's way…

Chapter 6 | Prayers When I need God's Guidance

Understanding the brevity of life
As I face each test,
I will trust You, Lord, with all my heart
That in all things You know best.

I believe whatever God has in store for us will be unbelievably more joyous, more delightful, and more wonderful that what we now enjoy.
– Billy Graham

God has an individual plan for each person. If you will go to Him and submit to Him, He will come into your heart and commune with you. He will teach and guide you in the way you should go.
– Joyce Meyer

Tears Within My Heart | K.M. Bowman

Acts 1: 8, "You shall receive power when the Holy Spirit has come upon you and you shall be My witnesses both in Jerusalem, and in all Judea and Samaria and even to the remotest part of the earth."

God's Work for Me

You say You will give me Your spirit, Lord,
That You are the source of power
To carry out the work You have for me
In this moment and in this hour…

It is others I want to serve
In the unique way You have designed for me,
I know You will show me clearly
Just what You want it to be…

You will not only show me what,
But You will also tell me where,
You will use me to share the story
Of Your great love, mercy, and care…

I am an instrument of Your love, Lord,
Asking to be filled with Your spirit today
That I might extend grace and mercy
To those You send my way.

Chapter 6 | Prayers When I need God's Guidance

The true and living God, the One who lives from eternity to eternity, desires more than anything that we humble ourselves and make Him our personal, one-and-only God. When we do that, He comes to us and lives within us, gives us direction, and teaches us His ultimate truth.
– Tony Evans

Philippians 1: 6 (NRSV), "Paul wrote, 'I am confident of this, that the one who began a good work among you will bring it to completion by the day of Jesus Christ.'"

II Timothy 1: 9, "Who hath saved us, and called us with an holy calling..."

How Am I Answering God's Call?

In my own life today, Lord,
How am I answering Your call?
I am not here for myself,
But for a ministry to all...

You have a purpose, Lord,
For each one of us here,
You are calling me now,
Is Your call to me clear?..

You set an example
Of serving others in love,
This is the mission
I should be obedient of...

May I listen closely and I'll hear
You speaking to me,
How am I answering Your call
In what You want me to be?

Chapter 6 | Prayers When I need God's Guidance

The place God calls you is the place where your deep gladness and the world's deep hunger meet.
– Frederick Buechner

All Christians are called to develop God-given talents, to make the most of their lives, to develop to the fullest their God-given powers and capacities.
– Henry Blackaby

Tears Within My Heart | K.M. Bowman

Mark 6:46, "And when He had sent them away, He departed into a mountain to pray."

How Many Times Have I Prayed Today?

How many times have I prayed today, Lord?
A short little minute span?
Or is my life one continuous prayer
Around which my life is planned?

You spent much time in daily prayer,
You were never too hurried to pray,
Your example's for me to spend much time in prayer
As I go about my day...

How important it is to meet You, Lord,
With perseverance and persistence and pleading,
Knowing that You hold the only key
To what my life is needing.

Chapter 6 | Prayers When I need God's Guidance

Prayer is for every moment of our lives, not just for times of suffering or joy.
– Billy Graham

There is no part of religion so neglected as private prayer.
– J. C. Ryle

Tears Within My Heart | *K.M. Bowman*

Ecc. 9: 10 (NKJV), "Whatever your hand finds to do, do it with your might."

If God Has Called You, "Go!"

If You call me, Lord, I will go,
When You open the door, I won't delay,
For I must be the right person for Your job,
I will follow Your leading today…

For the work, You will give me tools;
For instructions, You will show me how,
For location, You will take me there;
I will be obedient to You now…

Do I hear You calling me, Lord?
Yes, I hear Your voice and will obey,
For great blessings await my serving You,
Great blessings along the way.

Chapter 6 | Prayers When I need God's Guidance

God doesn't call the equipped. He equips the called.
God doesn't call the qualified. He qualifies the called.
 – Greg Albrecht

Tears Within My Heart | *K.M. Bowman*

II Chronicles 26:15, "His fame spread far and wide, for he was marvelously helped till he became strong."

Keep Me Humble, Lord

Keep me humble, Lord
In my life and work I do
So when things are going well
It's not me, but you...

It's you who makes me strong
It's you who blesses me
It's you who gives me confidence
In this, O let me see...

Nothing can I do
Without your help and guide
Keep me humble, Lord,
With you right by my side.

Chapter 6 | Prayers When I need God's Guidance

Humility is to make a right estimate of one's self.
– Charles H. Spurgeon

Very humble work, that is where you and I must be. For there are many people who can do big things. But there are very few people who will do the small things.
– Mother Teresa

Tears Within My Heart | K.M. Bowman

James 3: 13, "Who is wise and understanding among you? Let him show it by his good life, by deeds done in the humility that comes from wisdom.

Keep Me, Lord

Keep my eyes on You, O Lord,
Through every day and night,
And when the darkest skies may come,
You will make them bright...

Keep my feet on solid ground,
On paths of right for You,
My walk to bring You loving honor,
My steps Your work to do...

Keep my thoughts on You alone
That they may bring You glory,
Keep my heart strings pure within
As I share Your faith and story.

Chapter 6 | Prayers When I need God's Guidance

Faithfulness means continuing quietly with the job we have been given, in the situation where we have been placed; not yielding to the restless desire for change. It means tending the lamp quietly for God without wondering how much longer it has got to go on.
– Evelyn Underhill

Tears Within My Heart | K.M. Bowman

John 3:30, "He must increase, but I must decrease."

Lord, Teach Me to Be Humble

Lord, teach me to be humble,
That I might be small so You can be great,
That You may be known and honored,
That Your life I can imitate…

May I go unnoticed that You might be noticed,
May my greatest privilege be to magnify You,
May I decrease that You might increase,
May songs of exultation be my highest view…

Teach me, Lord, to be humble,
Small that You are great,
Large that You are my refuge,
Empty that a new heart You create…

Chapter 6 | Prayers When I need God's Guidance

When I survey the wondrous cross on which the Prince of Glory died, my richest gain I count but loss and pour contempt on all my pride.
– Isaac Watts

I believe the first test of a truly great man is humility.
– John Ruskin

Tears Within My Heart | *K.M. Bowman*

Matthew 16: 25, "Whoever loses his life for my sake will find it."

Lord, What Will You Have Me to Do?

Lord, what will you have me do this day,
This day that is now so new?
What is the work You assign me this day?
What is my work to do?

Will You have me to help someone who is older
Or a child who has gone astray?
What is the work You call me to do?
What is my work today?

Maybe it's shopping for groceries to help
Or cleaning one's home when they're ill,
Maybe to take in a cake or a pie
Or when sick to take in a meal...

I am here to serve You this day, O Lord,
To receive any assignment You give,
What is the work You will have me to do
To make another life easier to live?

Chapter 6 | Prayers When I need God's Guidance

Age, health, and stage in life have nothing to do with serving or not serving. In each season of life, there are attributes and qualities of life and experience that God values in service.
– Bruce Kemper

We are pilgrims on a journey, we are brothers on the road. We are here to help each other walk the mile and bear the load.
– Richard Gillard

> "But grow in grace, and in the knowledge of our Lord & Savior Jesus Christ."
> – II Peter 3:18

"Hang this question up in your houses: 'What would Jesus do?' For what Jesus would do and how He would do it, may always stand as the best guide to us."
– C.H. Spurgeon

Prayers When I Seek God's Leading

Chapter 7

Tears Within My Heart | K.M. Bowman

Mark 10: 51 (NRSV), "Jesus said to Bartimaeus, 'What do you want Me to do for you?'"

My Mission

My mission, O Lord,
Is to Your people give care,
To help meet their needs,
To minister in prayer...

In the midst of my journey,
May I hear their cry,
May I stop to help
As I pass them by...

As you healed blind Bartimaeus
On Your journey that day,
You saw an opportunity,
Not an interruption of dismay...

May I, like You,
Hear someone's cry
And be sensitive to help
As I, too, pass by...

For my mission, O Lord,
Is to Your people give care,
And to serve You through them
In an opportunity rare.

Chapter 7 | Prayers When I Seek God's Leading

If God's love is for anybody anywhere, it's for everybody everywhere.
– Edward Lawlor

We are prone to argue with the Lord against an assignment that seems to us difficult, dangerous, and impossible. But our part is to trust Him fully, to obey Him implicitly, and to follow His instructions faithfully.
– V. Raymond Edman

Tears Within My Heart | *K.M. Bowman*

Matthew 14:27 "Jesus spoke to them saying, 'Be of good cheer! It is I; do not be afraid.'"

My Purpose on Earth

I must move gently, move slowly
In this life on earth
Else I'll miss my purpose
And lose my worth....

My purpose on earth, Lord,
Is to serve You first,
Through the thick and thin
Through the best and worst...

Every day I will praise You,
And thank You I'm here
I'll believe You and trust You
And know that You're near...

I'll tell You I'm ready,
To serve those You send
Be they family or strangers,
Enemies or friends....

When I put You first, Lord,
It all falls into place,
And I'll go through life
With Your mercy and grace....

Chapter 7 | Prayers When I Seek God's Leading

When I stay in close communion,
You'll tell me what to do,
Life won't seem like a puzzle,
For You'll see me through...

May I walk gently each day
And when the unexpected hits,
You will keep me on course, Lord,
Like the rudder on a ship. ...

When I feel overwhelmed,
I'll stop awhile and think,
For You are standing there beside me
That I might not sink...

And through it all may I remember
That my purpose here on earth-
Is serving You first, Lord,
Through the best and the worst.

Do all the good you can, by all the means you can, in all the ways you can, in all the places you can, at all the times you can, to all the people you can, as long as ever you can.
– John Wesley

Deut. 5: 32, "Let me hear your voice behind me whenever I turn aside to the right or to the left."

Acts 16: 6, "Paul and his companions...were kept by the Holy Spirit from preaching the word in the province of Asia."

My Ways or God's?

Your ways alone are higher, Lord,
Than the ways my feet would take,
For You are perfect, infinite in power,
And You make no mistake...

When in doubt which way to turn,
I come to You and say,
"Please help me, Lord, close every door,
But the one You want today."

And there I am and there are You,
Stopping every step but Yours,
I hear Your voice behind me say,
"Go not the way that lures..."

"In me is life, in me are blessings,
My ways I will make plain,
When doors are shut, be obedient to me,
My way will be your gain."

Chapter 7 | Prayers When I Seek God's Leading

I know now which way to take,
I trust You, Lord, to lead,
Moving forward with a confident heart,
Obeying when You intercede.

All the works of God are unsearchable and unspeakable, no human sense can find them out.
– Martin Luther

When we hear His call and respond appropriately, there will be no limit to what God can and will do through His people. But if we do not even recognize when He is speaking, we are in trouble at the very heart of our relationship to Him.
– Henry Blackaby

You got to be careful if you don't know where you're going, because you might not get there.
– Yogi Berra

Tears Within My Heart | *K.M. Bowman*

II Tim. 2: 9, "I suffer trouble…even to the point of chains; but the word of God is not chained."

No Deed Is Too Small

Sometimes I feel I'm isolated, Lord,
With things beyond my control,
A hospital bed, losing my job,
An illness taking its toll…

Financially disadvantaged,
Being older and shut in,
May I find ways to reach out,
For You will guide me within…

When done for You, Lord,
No deed is too small,
Be it prayers or a note,
You use them all…

It might be my card
That gives someone cheer,
When the hope that was there
Had all disappeared…

Or encouraging words
Through a telephone call
Could lift a sad spirit
That it might not fall…

Chapter 7 | Prayers When I Seek God's Leading

*He was almost paralyzed,
He had a massive stroke,
Only a left eye blink
Was all he could provoke...

But with a coded alphabet,
And the blink of his eye,
He wrote a book
To help others survive...

The book required
About 200,000 blinks
The only physical ability
That to others he linked...

Humbly may I serve, Lord,
As in You I confide,
Knowing no deed is too small,
If You are glorified.

All service ranks the same with God.
– Robert Browning

---

*Jean-Dominique Bauby's memoir, THE DIVING AND THE BUTTERFLY–
His massive stroke left him with a condition called, "Locked in Syndrome."

Tears Within My Heart | K.M. Bowman

The service of the less gifted brother is as pure as that of the more gifted, and God accepts both with equal pleasure.
– A. W. Tozer

Matthew 2: 13, "Stay there until I tell you."

O Restless Heart

O restless heart, beating against the prison bars
Of my circumstances narrow and small,
I long for a wider path of service
Because there seems to be no life at all…

I am in the midst of monotony
Of my daily mundane routine,
I feel the work I am being given
Cannot be heard or seen…

Stand still and quiet, O restless heart,
For You, O Lord, have placed me there;
You have a reason for your work to do,
If I trust in Your guiding care…

I must trust Your wisdom, trust Your hand,
Giving You my earthly praise;
You know what's best for me to do,
When I allow You to direct my days…

Chapter 7 | Prayers When I Seek God's Leading

Who knows that You are preparing me, Lord,
For a far greater work You'll send,
And through my daily mundane work,
I can handle the job I'll tend...

So stay, O restless heart, where You have been carefully placed,
And Your work, Lord, let me faithfully do,
Till I hear Your gentle voice calling,
"Leave, I now have something greater for you."

Men in general would rather be somewhere else than where God in His providence has placed them.
– John Dawson

None of us ought to presume to question the circumstances of his existence. Whether good or bad, comfortable or awkward, opulent or Spartan, we may be certain that we live as we were decreed to live by a caring God. Therefore, all is well.
– Charles Doss

We can be content in Christ, regardless of our circumstances because in Him we have everything we need, for now and forever.
– Donald S. Whitney

Hebrews 5: 8-9, "Although He was a Son, He learned obedience from the things which He suffered. And having been made perfect, He became to all those who obey Him the source of eternal salvation."

Obedience

Am I obedient, Lord?
Do I follow Your way?
Or am I willful
And disobey?

Am I independent,
Wanting to be in control?
Is my life filled
With self-centeredness my goal?...

When I think about Jesus,
That's the way I should be,
He was obedient unto death
In the hour of Gethsemane...

I must submit my willfulness, Lord,
To someone greater than me,
Obeying Your instruction without understanding,
That is the key...

Do I have a stubborn streak, Lord?
Let me give it to You today,
For You know what is best
When Your will I obey...

What am I withholding from You, Lord?
What are You asking me to do?
Why am I resisting Your instruction?
May I be obedient and You will see me through.

The Christian man must aim at that complete obedience to God in which life finds its highest happiness, its greatest good, its perfect consummation, its peace.
– William Barclay

For the heart to obey Christ, the heart must be in Christ.
– F. B. Meyer

Tears Within My Heart | K.M. Bowman

Luke 12: 15, "A man's life does not consist in the abundance of his possessions."

Only My Daily Bread

Give me neither poverty nor riches, O Lord,
But only my daily bread,
With food and clothing I am content,
For by Your spirit I am fed...

Better the little of righteous, than the wealth of wicked,
I have learned along the way,
Just to be content with what I have
As I live my life each day...

In the abundance of his possessions, Lord,
A man's life does not consist,
But only in the knowledge of You,
And Your spirit can man subsist...

So neither poverty nor riches do I want, Lord,
But only my daily bread,
As I look to You for my life
And by Your hand I am daily fed.

Chapter 7 | Prayers When I Seek God's Leading

A soul that is capable of knowing God can be filled with nothing else but God.
– Jeremiah Burroughs

There is just one thing more I wish I could give you. It is the religion of our Lord Jesus Christ. With it, if you had nothing else, you could be happy. Without it, though you had all things else, you could not be happy.
– Patrick Henry

Tears Within My Heart | *K.M. Bowman*

Hebrews 4: 16, "Let us, therefore, come boldly unto the throne of grace that we may obtain mercy, and find grace to help in time of need."

Only One Moment

Help me, O Lord, to live in the moment,
This moment that's given to me,
Whether eating or sleeping, resting or working,
This moment that's meant to be...

Help me this moment others to serve
As I reach out in love from You,
May I receive mercy and find grace to help
Those You place in my view...

Lord, You have given me only one moment,
This is the moment now;
May I take this moment and use this moment
For You as I humbly bow.

Chapter 7 | Prayers When I Seek God's Leading

All my possessions for a moment of time.
– Queen Elizabeth I

Minutes are worth more than money. Spend them wisely.
– Thomas P. Murphy

No time for God? What fools we are...No time for God? As soon to say no time to eat, to sleep, to live, to die. Take time for God, or a poor misshapen thing you'll be to step into eternity, and say, "I had no time for Thee."
– Anonymous

Acts 16: 7, *"When they came to the border Mysia, they tried to enter Bithynia, but the spirit of Jesus would not allow them to."*

Romans 12: 12, *"Be joyful in hope, patient in affliction, faithful in prayer. Share with God's people who are in need. Practice hospitality."*

Only Wait

You opened the door, Lord,
Then You closed it again;
Are You not calling?
I do not understand...

My work seemed productive,
Yielding service for You,
Then You called me aside
For another work to do...

Sometimes You call, Lord,
To serve by staying still,
By doing nothing at all,
Or by waiting for Your will...

Sometimes You send opposition,
Forcing me to go back,
Sometimes You send sickness,
Increasing faith that I lack...

Chapter 7 | Prayers When I Seek God's Leading

I will not complain, Lord,
When You don't want me to go,
Patiently I'll wait
Till another way You show...

When called before Your door
And closed is the gate,
May I hear Your gentle whisper,
"I am working, ONLY WAIT."

We cannot eat the fruit while the tree is in blossom.
– Benjamin Disraeli

Be patient in little things. Learn to bear the everyday trials and annoyances of life quietly and calmly, and then, when unforeseen trouble or calamity comes, your strength will not forsake you.
– William Swan Plumer

He never shows up late; he knows just what is best; fret not yourself in vain; until He comes, just rest.
– Anonymous

Tears Within My Heart | *K.M. Bowman*

Psalm 46: 10-11, "Cease striving and know that I am God; I will be exalted among the nations; I will be exalted in the earth; the Lord of hosts is with us."

Our Lord Is in Control

In all things, Lord,
You are in control;
When I cease my striving,
You bring about Your goal...

In all my uncertainties,
And attempts to gain control,
Only You know, Lord,
How to make me whole...

I try to gain control,
I want to be secure,
But this is only an illusion,
For only You will endure...

My priority is to know You,
To worship You and be still,
For You have it under control,
Your plans You will fulfill...

You are exalted among the nations,
You are exalted in the earth,
You, O Lord, are with me;
You alone give me worth.

Chapter 7 | Prayers When I Seek God's Leading

Taking delight in random encounters that come our way is a wonderful reminder that God is in control.
– Mel Lawrenz

God is as near as your next breath and He is in control.
– Beth Moore

Titus 2: 7, "In everything set them an example by doing what is good."

People Are Watching Me

People are watching me;
How am I living this day?
They hear how I speak to my husband;
With my children, they observe their way...

They see me confront disappointments;
They observe as problems I face;
My prayer, Lord, is they'll see You in me
Showing Your mercy and grace...

They see me when going to work,
To church or the grocery store;
Each day may they see <u>You</u> in me,
Reflecting Your love more and more...

They know if I'm getting gas,
In the post office, bank, or ill,
Let them see peace and trust, O Lord,
As they watch my daily drill...

People are being helped, O Lord,
By observing the example of others,
May the example of seeing You in me
Bring goodness and love to one another...

Chapter 7 | Prayers When I Seek God's Leading

Help me be careful how I live,
For people are watching me,
As they observe my daily life, Lord,
Will <u>You</u> in me they see?

If I live by the human equivalents of grace, love, forgiveness and faith, with those who occupy space in my life, thinking more of belonging than of owning, seeking to maintain the relationship as a matter of supreme importance, those relationships will never grow "stale," but sweeter every day.
– Sandra W. Hoover

I will do nothing in this life except what I see is necessary, profitable, and salutary to my neighbor, since through faith I have an abundance of all good things in Christ.
– Martin Luther

This above all: to thine own self be true, and it must follow as the night the day, thou canst not then be false to any man.
– William Shakespeare

Example is not the main thing in influencing others. It is the only thing!
– Albert Schweitzer

Proverbs 21: 30, "There is no wisdom, no insight, no plan that can succeed against the Lord."

Psalm 32: 8, "I will instruct you and teach you in the way you should go; I will counsel you and watch over you."

The Leaf

I am just your driver, Lord,
Please tell me where to go,
Set my feet upon new roads
And help my spirit grow...

New adventures may I embrace;
New experiences with You;
New visions, Lord, of a greater service
You are calling me to do...

Like the leaf upon the water,
Floating gently in Your care,
Guide me on life's roads
That I Your love with others share.

Chapter 7 | Prayers When I Seek God's Leading

Life is the art of drawing without an eraser.
– John Christian

We are not told that we cannot plan ahead, just that we should not be dogmatic in our planning.
-Edith Schaeffer

Tears Within My Heart | K.M. Bowman

Psalm 46: 1-3, "God is our refuge and strength, a very present help in trouble. Therefore, we won't be afraid though the earth changes, though the mountains are shaken into the heart of the seas; though its waters roar and are troubled, though the mountains tremble with their swelling."

The Storm

The storm is here, O Lord,
The snow is coming down,
And hour by hour it is growing
Deeper on the ground...

The wind is picking up–
A blizzard now they say,
"Unsafe to travel, stay inside,"
Were words coming through today...

The storm has come upon me,
Distilled in all its wrath,
But through this storm of fury, Lord,
You will make a path...

A path for me to follow,
To keep me safe, secure,
The storm may rage in fury, Lord,
But with You, I will endure.

Chapter 7 | Prayers When I Seek God's Leading

A recognition of truth and the practice of virtue is the title to security for both the individuals and the whole of mankind.
– John of Salisbury

There is more safety with Christ in the tempest than without Christ in the calmest waters.
– Alexander Grosse

Security is not the absence of danger, but the presence of God no matter what the danger.
– Anonymous

> *"And the peace of God, which passeth all understanding, shall keep your hearts and minds through Christ Jesus."*
> *– Philippians 4:7*

"It is in loving, not in being loved, the heart is blessed; It is in giving, not in seeking gifts, we find our quest. Whatever be your longing or need, that give – so shall your soul be fed, and you, indeed, shall live."
– Anonymous

Prayers for Peace & Contentment

Chapter 8

Tears Within My Heart | K.M. Bowman

Deuteronomy 8: 17 (NRSV), "Do not say to yourself, 'My power and the might of my own hand have gotten me this wealth.'"

All That I Have

All that I have, Lord, comes from You,
My strength, my intelligence, my work to do,
All that You've created, all that I see,
Everything past, everything that will be,
My ability to work, the seeds that grow,
My gift of thinking, the knowledge I know;
My gift of love and how to relate,
The ability to forgive and to communicate,
My spirit, my attitude, my own good health,
My rest, my faith, the gift of wealth;
All that I have, Lord, comes from You,
Gifts of Your love as I journey through.

Chapter 8 | Prayers for Peace & Contentment

What I have today, I have because of His mercy. I did not earn it. I do not deserve it. I did not pay for it. I have no rights to it. I cannot keep it except for one thing—God's mercy.
– David Crosby

Tears Within My Heart | K.M. Bowman

Exodus 20: 17, "You shall not covet."

I Timothy 6: 6-7, "But godliness with contentment is great gain. For we brought nothing into this world, and it is certain we can carry nothing out."

All That I Need

You have given me, Lord,
All that I need,
You have made me wealthy,
Wealthy, indeed!...

Wealthy in family,
Wealthy in friends,
Wealthy in blessings
That never end...

Your love that goes with me
Forever and ever,
Your mercy surrounding me
That leaves me never...

When you have given me
All that I need,
You have made me rich, Lord,
Rich, indeed!...

Chapter 8 | Prayers for Peace & Contentment

May contentment follow me
In my journey here,
For You have given
All I need and hold dear.

Peace is not the absence of conflict but the presence of God no matter what the conflict.
– Anonymous

Charles Spurgeon tells of a farmer who has on the weather vane of his barn the motto, "God is love." He was asked if the motto was intended to suggest that God is as changeable as the wind. "Oh, no!" said the farmer. "It means that no matter which way the wind blows, 'God is love.'"

That is the secret of being content, the secret of a quiet heart.
– E. Brandt Gustavson

Isaiah 55: 12 NIV, "You will...be led forth in peace."

Do I Have Peace About It?

Whatever I'm facing, Lord,
Do I have the peace that I need?
If I don't have that peace,
Then I must not proceed...

Because the first thing I lose
When I step out of Your will
Is Your great peace
That no one understands still...

Many times only peace
Is what You will give
To let me know I'm on track
With the way I should live...

When it feels confusing, contradictory,
And nothing's going right,
Yet I'm able to remain calm,
Your peace, Lord, is my light...

That's Your peace which transcends
All my understanding, (Phil. 4: 7 NIV)
Your peace of calm within chaos,
A peace undemanding...

Chapter 8 | Prayers for Peace & Contentment

In my life, Lord, may I be at peace
After I suffer a little while,
For You will restore and strengthen me
To face every trial.

Nothing will or can restore order till our hearts make the great decision: God shall be exalted above all else.
– A. W. Tozer

The peace is won by accompanying God into the battle.
– Elvind Josef Berggrav

Isaiah 26: 3-4, "The steadfast of mind Thou will keep in perfect peace, because he trusts in Thee. Trust in the Lord forever for, in God the Lord, we have an everlasting Rock."

God's Perfect Peace

Your peace, O Lord, is perfect,
May I have that peace within,
A quiet, steadfast, perfect peace
That only You can send...

Sometimes it's hard to be steadfast
When interruptions come,
A broken stove, a car repair,
Countless errands to run...

But I want your perfect peace, O Lord,
I want to stay focused on you,
Help me trust and stay steadfast
With nothing else in view.

Chapter 8 | Prayers for Peace & Contentment

At the foot of my bed, where I can see it on retiring, and the first thing on arising, are these words: "Thou wilt keep him in perfect peace, whose mind is stayed on thee because he trusteth in thee." (Isaiah 26: 3)
– William Gladstone

John 16: 33 NASB, "These things I have spoken to you, so that in Me you may have peace. In the world you have tribulation, but take courage, I have overcome the world."

John 14: 27 NASB, "Peace I leave with you; my peace I give to you; not as the world gives do I give to you. Do not let your heart be troubled, nor let it be fearful."

Guideposts to Peace

What are the guideposts
On the footpath to peace
That will speak to my soul, Lord,
And my spirit release?

To be glad of life,
To find joy in today,
Because it gives me the chance
To love, work, and play...

To be content with my possessions,
But to know how to give,
To think seldom of my enemies,
And with my friends learn to live...

To keep my focus on You, Lord,
And my thoughts filled with praise,
To sing a song in my heart
Through all of my days...

Chapter 8 | Prayers for Peace & Contentment

To walk with You in Your world, Lord,
And see the things You have made,
To let Your wonder of creation
Fill every fiber You gave...

To remain free from worry
For You are in control–
You know how to lead–
What's best for my soul...

Find joy in the moment,
Calm in great needs,
And I'll be well on my way
Along the footpath to peace.

To be glad of life because it gives you the chance to love and to work and to play and to look up at the stars; to be satisfied with your possessions, but not contented with yourself until you have made the best of them; to despise nothing in the world except falsehood and meanness, and to fear nothing except cowardice; to be governed by your admirations rather than by your disgusts; to covet nothing that is your neighbor's except his kindness of heart and gentleness of manners; to think seldom of your enemies, often of your friends, and every day of Christ; and to spend as much time as you can, with body and with spirit, in God's out-of-doors–these are little guideposts on the footpath to peace.
– Henry Van Dyke

Psalm 23: 1, "The Lord is my shepherd; I shall not want."

Hebrews 13: 5, "Keep your lives free from the love of money and be content with what you have, because God has said, "Never will I leave you; never will I forsake you."

I Shall Not Want

The things I have now
Are the things I once dreamed of,
But how happy am I?
For the greatest is love…

Lasting joy is not what I drive,
What I deposit, or where I dwell;
When You are my Shepherd, Lord,
I find all is well…

What I have in You, Lord,
Is much greater than
What I don't have in life
Which lasts only a span…

May I not wish for more things
For they will never replace
Your infinite love, Lord,
Which is always first place…

Chapter 8 | Prayers for Peace & Contentment

Money changes hands, changes thoughts,
Changes lives, changes what I see,
May I be sure through it all, Lord,
That it doesn't change me...

"I shall not want," Lord,
Are four words to live by,
For when You are my Shepherd,
You are my only supply.

He is a wise man who does not grieve for the things which he has not, but rejoices for those which he has.
– Epictetus

No matter how hard we work or how big our earthly treasure is, this life is never going to be enough. It will never be perfect, so there will never be the perfect time for us to sit down and relax.
-Susan Reedy

Tears Within My Heart | *K.M. Bowman*

John 4: 34, "Jesus said unto them, 'My meat is to do the will of Him that sent Me and to finish His work.'"

Living in Your Will, O Lord

Living in Your will, O Lord,
Is life's most important goal,
For living outside Your perfect will
I could lose my very soul...

I can have very little within Your will
And have peace within my heart,
I can have much living outside Your will
And be miserable from the start...

I can have joy in obscurity
If I am within Your will,
But be wretched with wealth and fame
In pursuit of selfish thrill...

I can be happy in the midst of suffering,
Knowing I have Your will within,
But have agony in good health
When I follow the way of sin...

When I am in Your will, O Lord,
I can be content, though poverty abounds,
But be destroyed by all my riches
When outside Your will resounds...

Chapter 8 | Prayers for Peace & Contentment

When I live within Your perfect will
In persecution I have calm and peace,
In acclaim when living outside Your will,
I suffer failure and decrease...

The most important thing of all, O Lord
Is living within Your will,
To follow Your sovereign mighty call
And Your divine plan fulfill.

The will of God prevails. In great contests, each party claims to act in accordance with the will of God. Both may be, and one must be, wrong. God cannot be for and against the same things at the same time
– Abraham Lincoln

God always gives us enough strength, and sense enough, for everything He wants us to do.
– John Ruskin

Tears Within My Heart | *K.M. Bowman*

Psalm 73: 25-26 (ESV), "Whom have I in heaven but You? And there is nothing on earth that I desire besides You. My flesh and my heart may fail, but God is the strength of my heart and my portion forever."

Longing for You, Lord

I'm longing for You, Lord,
I'm longing for <u>You</u>
To be my everything
To see me through…

My flower at dawn,
My sun so bright,
My sunset in evening,
My star in the night…

My song in the dark,
My dance in the light,
When I am weak,
My power and might…

For to You, I am Yours,
To You I belong,
You fill me with strength,
You make me strong…

Humble am I, Lord,
And resigned to Your will,
Fitted for doing,

Chapter 8 | Prayers for Peace & Contentment

And for Your suffering still...
I'm longing for You, Lord,
I'm longing for <u>You</u>
To be my everything
To see me through.

When life is going well, when material blessings are abundant, we tend to think that we're self-sufficient, that we don't need God. But when we realize the precariousness of life, we find ourselves more humble, more dependent, and more grateful.
– Pastor Kelly Peters

With God, there is no mutual ground; one chooses to be Godly or Worldly.
– Rev. Daniel Wegrzyn

Tears Within My Heart | *K.M. Bowman*

Psalm 25: 4-5, "Show me Your ways, O Lord, teach me Your paths; guide me in Your truth and teach me, for You are my God, my Savior, and my hope is in You all day long."

More Than Enough

More than enough, Lord,
You are to me,
More than enough,
You will always be...

More than the things
That round me lie,
More than possessions
That money can buy...

More than desires
Of being famous and free,
More than the wealth
Of living affluently...

More than position,
Power and praise,
More than career
That fills all my days...

More than enough, Lord,
You are to me,
More than enough,
You will always be!

Chapter 8 | Prayers for Peace & Contentment

When you have Christ, you are rich and have enough.
– Thomas a Kempis

O soul, He only who created thee can satisfy thee. If those ask for anything else, it is thy misfortune, for He alone who made thee in His image can satisfy thee.
– Augustine

Tears Within My Heart | K.M. Bowman

Psalm 46: 5 (NASB), "God is in the midst of her, she will not be moved; God will help her when morning dawns."

John 16: 33, "I have told you these things, so that in me you may have peace. In the world you will have trouble. But take heart! I have overcome the world."

Peace

Can I have the kind of peace, Lord,
Unshaken by factors without?
The kind of peace immovable–
Unshaken by wavering doubt?

Can I cling to You in trust,
Unmoved by earthly things?
Where nothing can upset me,
No matter what life brings?

Can I like Paul say, (Acts 20: 23, 24)
"But none of these things move me"?
Neither life nor possessions of earth
Can transcend Your authority...

Though disasters come on all sides,
There can be peace in view,
Peace transcending understanding
When I learn, Lord, to rest in You.

Chapter 8 | Prayers for Peace & Contentment

Peace is to be able to rest serenely in the storm!
– Billy Graham

Peace is not an absence of war, it is a virtue, a state of mind, a disposition for benevolence, confidence, justice.
– Benedict Spinoza

Tears Within My Heart | *K.M. Bowman*

Isaiah 26: 3, "Thou wilt keep him in perfect peace whose mind is stayed on Thee."

Perfect Peace

You keep me in perfect peace, O Lord,
When I turn my focus on You,
Even when my greatest concern
Or worry comes surfacing through...

With my mind centered completely on You,
Concerns of this world pass away,
Until nothing at all but perfect peace
Is left in my heart to stay...

Once under a busy railroad track
Was a little thrush's nest,
She peacefully, quietly sat on her eggs,
Undisturbed by the strain and stress...

Can I like the thrush find that kind of peace,
Knowing, Lord, You carry my cares?
Knowing You hear my plaintiff cry?
Knowing You answer my prayers?

When I turn my focus on You, O Lord,
You keep me in perfect peace,
And in You I find Your abundant grace
For my trials and burdens to release.

Chapter 8 | Prayers for Peace & Contentment

God is the whole reason we live, and knowing Him is to be our goal, not social approval or glandular satisfaction. He knows our needs; He has sent us a Comforter. And a life developed cheerfully and fully in the way God intended will bring the rewards that only God can give.
– Barbara Sroka

No tongue can tell the depth of that calm which comes over the soul which has received the peace of God which passeth all understanding.
– Charles Spurgeon

Tears Within My Heart | *K.M. Bowman*

Psalm 4: 8, "I will lie down and sleep in peace, for you alone, O Lord, make me dwell in safety."

Take What Each Day Brings

May I take what each day brings, Lord,
And bear it with a smile,
Some things might bring joys;
Others might bring trials...

It's all in how I see it
That makes or breaks my day;
If I see it with a smile,
Then things will go my way...

So may I take what each day brings, Lord,
And bear it with a smile;
You will bless me for it
And give me what's worthwhile.

Chapter 8 | Prayers for Peace & Contentment

Peace begins with a smile—smile five times a day at someone you don't really want to smile at, at all—do it for peace.
– Mother Teresa

A soul divided against itself can never find peace. Peace cannot exist where there are contrary loyalties. For true peace there has to be psychological and moral harmony. Conscience must be at rest.
– Hubert van Zeller

Matthew 6: 10 NKJF, "Your kingdom come, Your will be done."

The Breaking Process

It's the breaking process, Lord,
That I find I must go through,
To let <u>you</u> be in control
Of the things that I do…

Not to destroy my will,
But to re-direct my will,
Not to rob me of self-worth,
But to know You're my worth still…

Gideon's three hundred soldiers
Their pitchers had to break,
So light within could shine out,
And their enemies they could take… (Judges 7)

Elisha had to break his plow,
Representing his being financially secure,
Before receiving Your double portion, Lord,
To help His spirit endure… (I Kings 19: 19-21)

Mary had to break her alabaster box,
Filled with marriage expectations,
And with repentance and discipline,
Receive Christ's highest commendation… (Mark 14: 3-9)

Chapter 8 | Prayers for Peace & Contentment

Brokenness is costly!
It will change my very soul,
To submit my spirit to You, Lord,
And to know You are in control...

It happens through repentance, discipline and intimacy,
Repentance–the forgiveness of sin;
Discipline–to know You are in control;
Intimacy–praying from within...

Then let the breaking process begin,
Be in control, Lord, of my life today,
That I might have peace passing all understanding–
Peace in my heart to stay.

The Bible teaches that genuine repentance is evidenced by a change in behavior.
-Robert Jeffress

Tears Within My Heart | K.M. Bowman

Philippians 4: 7, "And the peace of God, which passeth all understanding shall keep your hearts and minds through Christ Jesus."

The Dying Embers of the Setting Sun

The dying embers of the setting sun
Are announcing the close of day,
A robin sings the song of dusk
As the embers fade away…

Darkness falls, the shadows come,
A peace settles over all,
You are there, Lord, with comfort and assurance
As night time comes to call…

I feel Your presence; I see Your work,
At the end of another day;
I sing Your praise and proclaim Your ways
For Your strength along the way.

Chapter 8 | Prayers for Peace & Contentment

Faith brings great ease of mind and perfect peace of heart.
– E. M. Bounds

We experience peace as we focus our thoughts and our vivid imaginations on the Father–and not on our concerns and worries.
– Gigi Graham Tchividjian

Tears Within My Heart | K.M. Bowman

Job 34: 29 (KJV), "He giveth quietness."

Exodus 33: 14, "My presence shall go with you and I will give you rest."

You Giveth Quietness

You giveth quietness, Lord, (Job 34: 29 KJV)
Not chaos, wind, and storm;
You giveth quietness
Into which the seed of peace is born…

Amid the noise and frenzied pace,
Amidst the turmoil, strain, and stress,
You giveth quietness and peace;
You giveth quietness and rest…

Amid my challenges far too great,
Amid my daunting tasks to face,
You giveth quietness,
You giveth mercy, peace, and grace…

I am desperate to know you're with me, Lord,
That You are with me in this place?
"My presence shall go with you," (Ex. 33: 14)
Is Your promise through all my days…

Chapter 8 | Prayers for Peace & Contentment

You giveth quietness, Lord,
You giveth me peace and rest
Within my trials and struggles
To withstand my present test.

God often speaks quietly, which suggests we need to be very still in order to hear him.
– Bob Buford

We hunger for quiet times; we find in them a womb to renew our strength.
– Virginia Ann Frole

Psalm 46: 10-11, "Cease striving and know that I am God. I will be exalted in the earth. The Lord of hosts is with us."

I Corinthians 7: 15, "God has called us to live in peace."

Your Peace Is Certain, Lord

Your peace is certain, Lord,
May I cease striving and know
That Your peace is powerful
When I surrender and let go…

What am I trying to control?
The outcome of my day?
How people perceive me?
Whether friends go or stay?

Your peace is comforting
As I remain still,
For You are in control
When I surrender my will.

Chapter 8 | Prayers for Peace & Contentment

We should have great peace if we did not busy ourselves with what others say and do.
– Thomas A. Kempis

Jesus Christ is the very center of my life, and knowing Him has brought a peace and joy that no words can describe.
– Susan Wheeler

www.ingramcontent.com/pod-product-compliance
Lightning Source LLC
Chambersburg PA
CBHW061637040426
42446CB00010B/1466